MW01064657

THE BIG BOOK OF

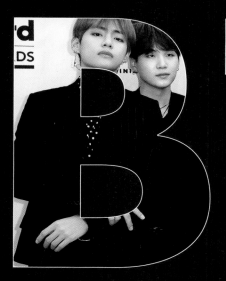

THE BIG BOOK OF
BTS

KATY SPRINKEL

Copyright © 2019 by Katy Sprinkel

No part of this publication may be reproduced, stored in a retrieval system, or transmitted in any form by any means, electronic, mechanical, photocopying, or otherwise, without the prior written permission of the publisher, Triumph Books LLC, 814 North Franklin Street, Chicago, Illinois 60610.

This book is available in quantity at special discounts for your group or organization. For further information, contact:

Triumph Books LLC
814 North Franklin Street
Chicago, Illinois 60610
(312) 337-0747
www.triumphbooks.com

Printed in U.S.A.

ISBN: 978-1-62937-759-9

Content written, developed, and packaged by Katy Sprinkel
Edited by Laine Morreau
Design and page production by Patricia Frey
Cover design by Preston Pisellini

All chapter-opening photos courtesy of Getty Images, except for photo of Suga, courtesy of Newscom. Photographs on pp. 1, 5, 6, 11, 12, 14, 17, 23, 28, 34, 38, 41, 46, 52, 59, 60, 64, 79, 81, 84, 87, 90, 93, 96, 99, 102, 105, 108, 115, 134, 137, 140, 143, 144, 147, 148, 151, 152, 155, 159, 168, 171 (top, second from top), 175, 178, 179, 187, 189, 191, and 192 courtesy of Getty Images. Illustrations and photographs on pages 70 and 171 (third from top, bottom) courtesy of iStock. Photographs on pp. 20, 27, 33, 50, 63, 66, 69, 74, 111, 117, 121, 156, 162, 165, 169, 170, 177, 180, and 184 courtesy of Newscom. Graphic on p. 54 courtesy of the author.

This book is not authorized, approved, or endorsed by BTS or Big Hit Entertainment. It is not an official publication.

CONTENTS

NO FALSE
IDOLS

If you haven't heard of BTS, maybe you've been asleep for the last few years...or hiding under a rock...or without a reliable Internet connection. If any of those scenarios apply to you, then consider this a formal introduction. The seven-member band known alternately as BTS or the Bangtan Boys is nothing short of a global phenomenon. And after years of making noise in their native South Korea, Japan, and beyond, the group is finally poised to make their biggest leap yet into the American mainstream.

They have had seven songs chart on the Billboard Hot 100 singles list (two of them in the top 10), have debuted three consecutive albums at No. 1 on the Billboard 200 albums chart, and have held the top spot on Billboard's Social 50 chart for all but nine weeks in the past *three*

BEST R&B ALBUM

BTS presents the award for Best R&B Album at the 2019 Grammy Awards ceremony. "Thank you to all our fans for making this dream come true, and we'll be back," promised RM.

Looking fly during a visit to SiriusXM in New York in 2019.

"If you haven't heard of BTS yet, it's time to succumb to the inevitable: The Korean boy band is taking over the world." —CNN

years. They've graced the cover of *Billboard* magazine (actually, seven of them—one cover for each of BTS's seven members), *Entertainment Weekly*, *Rolling Stone*, and even *Time*. In June 2018 they became the first group who doesn't record primarily in English to hit No. 1 on Billboard's Top 100 Artists chart as the top-selling artist in the U.S. What's more, they have a devoted legion of fans who earned them the Top Social Artist award at the Billboard Music Awards for three years running, besting the likes of Justin Bieber, Ariana Grande, Selena Gomez, and Shawn Mendes. And yet despite all that, they're still not yet a household name.

While chart performance and media recognition are all fine and good, they don't tell anywhere near the full story of BTS. Having already broken the mold in the hugely successful genre of K-pop, BTS is the first legitimate crossover success in the States. Why? Their unique brand of socially conscious pop/hip-hop music, slick choreography, and unprecedented fan engagement has set them apart from the rest of their contemporaries. Their self-dubbed "ARMY" of fans is a force to be reckoned with.

Formed in 2013, BTS (aka the Bangtan Boys, Bangtan Sonyeondan, the Bulletproof Boy Scouts, and the more recent

BTS burns up the stage at the 2017 American Music Awards.

moniker Beyond the Scene) is a seven-man group consisting of rappers RM, Suga, and J-Hope and vocalists Jin, V, Jimin, and Jungkook. Together, the multitalented Bangtan Boys have seamlessly blended their skills to create a unique K-pop group. Focusing on issues beyond the typical dance-pop offerings, BTS struck an immediate chord with fans.

Let's get one thing straight first: BTS is no fly-by-night operation. They are nothing less than international superstars. Since making their debut in 2013, they've been absolutely killing it in their native South Korea—they're the best-selling musical group in the country and have won South Korea's top artist prize for the last three years running. (They've also hit No. 1 in 73 other countries, thank you very much.)

They've won seemingly *every* award in South Korea, and have nabbed Billboard Music Awards, American Music Awards, and dozens of other awards in the U.S. and internationally. They even snagged their first Grammy nomination in 2019.

They're the most sought-after pitchmen in South Korea—the face of several brands, including Puma, Hyundai, LG Electronics, and even Coca-Cola, for which they represented South Korea at the 2018 World Cup, perhaps the world's biggest advertising stage.

More important, they're fearless activists and agents of change (*Rolling Stone* called them "K-pop's biggest taboo breakers"), whose music fearlessly tackles an array of social issues. They're global ambassadors for UNICEF and have even addressed the United Nations General Assembly.

BTS mania is so widespread that it's been compared to the likes of Beatlemania. (*The Late Show with Stephen Colbert* even paid homage to the Fab Four when BTS recently performed in *Colbert*'s Ed Sullivan Theater dressed in slim-cut black suits like the Beatles wore on their American TV debut 55 years earlier on the very same stage.) The band is riding an unprecedented wave of success around the world, and that wave is just now crashing on American shores. So if you aren't already certified ARMY, get prepared to become a new recruit! ♦

American fans often arrive at shows with messages written in Korean.

2

HALLYU
101

Fire! BTS in 2018.

To best appreciate what BTS has achieved, a little context might be helpful. So first, a little history. To the outside observer, K-pop looks like a sugarcoated confection, a frenetic collection of beats, catchy hooks, super-sharp dancing, and kaleidoscopic visuals performed by impossibly attractive singers and entertainers. But to dismiss it as a cotton-candy version of pop music would be way off the mark. Not only is K-pop wide-ranging in its musical styles and onstage product, it's serious business. Big business.

In fact, it is nearly impossible to overestimate the power of K-pop. The multibillion-dollar industry (that's right, *billion* with a *B*) is one of South Korea's biggest exports, and a huge contributor to the country's bottom line. Those eye-popping numbers are pretty impressive for a country with a population of only 51 million. (Compare that to the U.S.'s 326 million people.) In fact, South Korea "is the world's eighth-largest market for recorded music by revenue, according to the International Federation of the Phonographic Industry," Bloomberg reports. What's more, that's bigger than India (whose own entertainment industry is well-known worldwide) and even China. (And for those of you doing the math, India and China are the two most populous countries in the world, with more than 1.3 billion citizens apiece.)

So how did Korean culture become so pervasive? Let's rewind to the mid-20th century. In the aftermath of the Korean War, the country's ruler, President Park Chung-hee, supported strict cultural conservatism. (This included such "standards" as enforcing short haircuts on men and modest hemlines on women's clothing.) Additionally, the government controlled the media, so all radio and television programming was under its purview. The end result in music was an especially bland mixture of inoffensive, by-the-numbers pop music alongside traditional Korean music, known as *trot* (short for *foxtrot*).

BTS performs at KCON 2016 in Newark, New Jersey.

When South Korea became the so-called Sixth Republic in 1987, becoming a liberal democracy, things started to relax a little bit. One of the most popular television formats in South Korea at that time (and still today) was the musical competition show. Forebears to Western programs such as *American Idol* and *The X Factor*, Korea's weekly music shows—such as *Inkigayo* and *Music Bank*—were nothing less than appointment television. (And in a country where 99 percent of homes had a TV by the late 1980s, that's saying something.) Audiences were hugely invested in the outcomes.

Enter Seo Taiji and Boys. On April 11, 1992, the trio performed on the MBC network's weekly talent show. The song they performed, "Nan Arayo" ("I Know"), contained a lot of elements that would have been familiar to Americans at that time but were wholly unfamiliar to local Korean audiences. The song was seemingly influenced by the new jack swing style popularized in the early 1990s by groups Bell Biv DeVoe and Bobby Brown, among others. The unusual performance rocked the panel—but not in a good way. Seo Taiji and Boys received the lowest possible rating from the judges. The band didn't win the competition, or even the day, but they did something far more lasting. They lit the spark that ignited the K-pop explosion. Their performance had a profound influence on musicians who began to expand their sound beyond the predictable, staid formula popular in South Korea at the time. Unequivocally, this 1992 performance is considered to be the official beginning of K-pop as we know it today.

When the Asian financial crisis swept across the continent in 1997,

by the NUMBERS

$4.7 BILLION. According to the Korea Creative Content Agency, K-pop revenues in 2016, including marketing and licensing, totaled more than $4.7 billion. That's a pretty penny!

South Korea appeared to be on the brink of bankruptcy. New president Kim Dae-jung made a bold move in 1998, investing heavily in South Korea's entertainment industry as a means of saving the country from collapse.

The gambit worked. Korean music became popular in China as soon as it hit the airwaves there. And when Korean shows landed on Japanese television screens, viewers couldn't get enough. International audiences' obsession with Korean entertainers had an enormous ripple effect, and the craze for all things Korean became all-encompassing.

They call it *hallyu*—the Korean Wave—and it describes the influence of Korean culture on consumers. It encompasses not just music but television and movies, business, fashion, beauty, and even cuisine. (It sounds outlandish, but it's not inaccurate to say that the international rise in popularity of K-pop and Korean television (K-drama) has created opportunities for people around the world to buy Samsung phones and pick up kimchi at their local grocery stores.) The term *hallyu* was initially coined by Chinese journalists looking to describe the immense effect Korean culture exhibited on Chinese pop culture. The word was subsequently

pop QUIZ

Q: What's considered the epicenter of *hallyu* culture?
A: That's right, it's the Gangnam district of Seoul, as Psy made popular in his 2012 song "Gangnam Style."

adopted by the South Korean government as a badge of honor and a tool for promoting both industry and tourism.

The wave of *hallyu* grew stronger and stronger. But despite K-pop's giant popularity in Japan, China, and places as far-flung as Brazil, Australia, and Mexico, the music still had not seen a major breakthrough in the U.S. (Except for outlier Psy, whose 2012 smash "Gangnam Style" was a record-breaking commercial success but is now relegated to a footnote at best, a novelty song at worst.)

Until now, that is. And it's fitting that the reigning kings of K-pop,

BTS, are the ones to break into the American market. For one thing, their fan base is young, energetic, and millions strong. The group has collaborated with hugely successful American artists, from the Chainsmokers to Nicki Minaj to Halsey…with even more collaborations in the works. And unlike many K-pop performers, their music and lyrics dig a little deeper. It's pop music with a message, something that really connects with listeners.

And though Columbia Records distributes their music in North America, they have no plans of releasing an all–English language

Seo Taiji performs in this 2009 file photo.

great moments in HALLYU

—**1986** Censorship laws are repealed; Korean music flourishes
—1987
—**1988** Foreign travel ban is lifted; tourism soars
—1989
—1990
—1991
—1992
—1993
—1994
—1995
—1996
—**1997** President Kim Dae-jung bets big on entertainment
—1998
—**1999** Korea-set spy thriller *Swiri* is released
—**2000** *Autumn in My Heart* is released
—2001
—**2002** *Winter Sonata* premieres in Japan
—2003
—2004
—2005
—2006
—2007
—2008
—2009
—2010
—2011 ⎰Psy's "Gangnam Style" hits 1 billion YouTube views
—**2012**⎨First KCON is held in the U.S.
—2013 ⎱Samsung becomes No. 1 cell phone company
—2014
—2015
—**2016** *My Love from Another Star* premieres in China
—2017
—**2018** South Korea hosts the Winter Olympics
—**2019** BTS is first Asian artist to win BBMA's Best Duo/Group

Kim Dae-jung

Psy

2018 Olympic Games

album with the label. "If we sing suddenly in full English, and change all these other things, then that's not BTS," RM told *Entertainment Weekly*. And it's their authenticity that has set them apart from their K-pop peers. (More on that later.) Of the seven members, only RM speaks fluent English, though the remaining six are learning English and Japanese to better communicate with their biggest fan groups overseas. Given their massive success worldwide, it's safe to say that their music has a distinct universality. "Even if there is a language barrier, once the music starts, people react pretty much the same wherever we go," Suga told *Time*. "It feels like the music really brings us together." Jimin echoed the sentiment in 2019, once again shutting down rumors of an English-language effort: "Even if the [Korean] language is difficult,

we hope people understand the passion in our songs," Jimin said.

In the wake of their unprecedented success, the members of BTS have become the official poster boys of the Korean Wave. Case in point: in 2018 BTS became the first-ever idol group to be nominated for the prestigious Korean Popular Culture & Arts Award, recognized for their contributions to music but also for the huge impact they've had on the country's economy and tourism industry. They are South Korea's official tourism ambassadors, and according to a study done by the Hyundai Research Institute, 1 in 13 tourists to South Korea said they visited because of BTS.

Hallyu is indeed big business, both at home and abroad, and BTS is by far its biggest commodity. ◆

THE
FANTASY
FACTORY

Seo Taiji and Boys might not have received immediate acclaim for their innovation, but no one could say they didn't get attention. Their 1992 performance was something completely and utterly new, and it polarized audiences, who had never before seen a mash-up of Korean and American music. They were sharply criticized by some who objected to their use of hip-hop beats and rhythms (now the stock in trade of K-pop). They also committed such unforgivable sins as sporting dreadlocked hair and wearing bleached and ripped jeans.

Despite such trespasses, the song "Nan Arayo" ultimately became a huge hit at home—it reigned for 17 weeks as the No. 1 song in the country—and Seo Taiji and Boys established themselves as a massive idol group. They rode a tidal wave of success in the following four years, all the while experimenting with a wide range of musical genres, from hip-hop and rap styles popular over the American airwaves at that time to the softer, sweeter R&B balladeering of U.S. artists such as K-Ci & JoJo and Babyface.

EXO performs in concert in Hong Kong on Monday, June 2, 2014.

SHINee performs on KBC's Show Champion in 2013.

by the NUMBERS

$3 MILLION. That's the estimated cost of training one idol, according to a 2012 *Wall Street Journal* report.

The reason why Seo Taiji and Boys are considered the first K-pop band is that they literally blew up the system. Before then, most Korean pop music was wildly similar. By creating a new sound, they opened the door for other artists to find their own. Today, Korean groups are extremely open to experimentation and changing their sound, mashing up different influences. Which is why fans don't really consider K-pop to be a genre of music because there's no one identifiable sound. Instead, it's all about the full experience: the music, the live performance, the videos, the variety/competition shows,

and the physical packaging of the musical product.

"Rather than approach K-pop as a genre, a better approach would be 'integrated content,'" Suga told a Grammy Museum audience in 2019. "K-pop includes not just the music but the clothes, the makeup, the choreography…. All these elements I think sort of amalgamate together in a visual and auditory content package. That I think sets it apart from other music or maybe other genres."

Before Seo Taiji and Boys, music was ostensibly minted by the broadcasting companies, who promoted their own on-air products. But this group wrote, produced, and choreographed everything on their own. And because of their success, they upended the status quo. With it, a new studio production company system was born.

When the band broke up in 1996, one of the "Boys"–Yang Hyun-suk–joined the production fray, founding YG Entertainment. (The YG comes from his nickname, Yang-gun.) The YG agency is one of the so-called "Big Three" entertainment companies in South Korea, along with JYP Entertainment and SM Entertainment (which were also founded by former musicians). Together they dominate the musical landscape in Korea and produce the lion's share of K-pop music, and their reach is enormous.

Ask any K-pop fan, and they could tell you about each label's hallmarks. Listeners are loyal to their chosen label, much as sports

fans stay true to their team's colors. Since its inception in 1995, SM has been the leader of the pack. Home to hundreds of artists, it's known for its performance-oriented focus (meaning big visuals, sharp choreography, and catchy, danceable tunes). JYP is known for its polished trainee program and diverse class of recruits, turning out some of the most well-rounded musicians of the bunch. YG, like its founder, produces artists who tend to push musical boundaries and who possess an edgier look than their competitors.

Rather than focusing on grooming a select number of artists for long-term success, these companies churn out a multitude of acts, a seemingly revolving door for bands. The metrics for success are simply different in the K-pop system, where a band's shelf life may only be two years. This span is

the BIG THREE vs. BIG HIT

Call it the little engine that could. BTS label Big Hit Entertainment earned $196 million in 2018, overtaking behemoth JYP Entertainment to become the third-highest in sales revenue among Korean labels. That's massive news considering the long-established Big Three labels handle numerous acts while BTS is by and large the sole earner for Big Hit.

	SM Entertainment	YG Entertainment	JYP Entertainment	Big Hit Entertainment
Founder	Lee Soo-man	Yang Hyun-suk	Park Jin-young	Bang Si-hyuk
Operating since	1995	1996	1997	2005
Known for	Strict training regimen	Songwriting	Culturally and musically diverse artists	Allowing their flagship group, BTS, to have total artistic freedom
Biggest acts	S.E.S., H.O.T., SHINee, Girls' Generation, BoA, EXO, Super Junior	Big Bang, Blackpink, iKON, 2NE1	TWICE, 2PM, Wonder Girls, Rain, Miss A, San E	BTS, Homme, Lee Hyun
Milestone	First-generation K-pop band H.O.T. makes it big	Psy's "Gangnam Style" becomes an international phenomenon	TWICE and former Miss A member Suzy propel the agency to No. 2 in earnings among the Big Three	BTS shakes up the establishment, becoming a phenomenon at home and abroad
Also dabbles in...	Film, TV, theater, and even a travel agency	TV, apparel, cosmetics, and sports	Film, TV, restaurants, games, and even operates a business school	TV; he has been likened to Simon Cowell for his critical judging style on music shows

Jimin takes center stage at the 2017 AMAs.

what's the WORD?

bang song
Meaning "broadcast," it refers to the weekly music shows that are hugely influential in shaping the Korean musical landscape.

dictated by a couple things: First, the emphasis on youth. Since image is an essential component of the K-pop look, many artists age out of the system quickly. And for boy groups, things are also complicated by age in another way. All male citizens in South Korea must serve two years in the military, entering a draft at age 18.

Performers start early, auditioning as young as 9 or 10 years old. Foreign language fluency is prized in trainees, and native English speakers are a sought-after commodity. Once individuals are recruited by an agency and signed to long-term contracts, their formal training begins. Children are schooled during the day—a curriculum that includes a heavy dose of foreign language training, particularly Chinese, Japanese, and English. Then, once the school day is over, students start their music training—singing, dancing, and even media training. This is not for the faint of heart; a typical day begins early in the morning and stretches until 8:00 or 9:00 PM, before students return to their dormitories to complete their day's homework.

The performers will spend years as trainees before they are finally brought to market, only premiering once they have mastered their performances down to every hand gesture and eye wink. No detail is overlooked. But the breakneck pace doesn't let up any after their debut. Groups tour extensively, promote exhaustively, and are often tabbed for endorsement deals that require appearances and other promotional efforts. As Tiffany Chan writes on Medium.com, "These South Korean stars represent much more than their latest album…they uphold the image of an ideal in South Korean society, perfectly in-sync choreography, strong vocal talent, and exceptionally attractive visuals."

The companies also take charge of creating and distributing fan chants, which are another essential part of the live shows. Fans will have what amounts to a script. Instead of vocal backing tracks, live performances are enhanced by precisely crafted audience chants. Most songs have them, and it makes regular callbacks look like child's play. (Case in point: BTS's fan chants are disseminated, discussed, and practiced exhaustively by ARMYs.)

Then there's the music. Groups are expected to release songs early and often. In contrast to the American record industry, groups announce their releases only a few weeks in advance, drop the EP or album, then start the process all over again. Typically, a K-pop group will release music throughout the calendar year.

And that music is almost always accompanied by a music video, an essential part of the K-pop formula. These videos are invariably lavishly produced affairs that feature the requisite come-hither stares from idol group members but also showcase the groups' onstage prowess. The music videos prominently feature choreographed dance routines, which accompany each song and are an integral part of a single's identity. The past two

Performing in New York's Central Park as a part of Good Morning America's summer concert series.

know your IDOLS

Here are a handful of artists from K-pop's glittering past.

g.o.d.
One of the earliest K-pop groups, g.o.d. (short for Groove Over Dose) remains one of the genre's best-selling artists. >> Listen to this: "Lies"

BoA
The Korean Queen of Pop's multilingual chops made her a bona fide international success. >> Listen to this: "Valenti"

S.E.S.
The first successful girl group of the K-pop era, S.E.S. (taking its initials from members Sea (Bada), Eugene, and Shoo) traded their good-girl image for a more provocative look over the years. >> Listen to this: "I'm Your Girl"

Rain
Solo artist and actor Rain became one of K-pop's first international success stories. >> Listen to this: "Rainism"

Wonder Girls
They made a splash in the U.S., opening on tour for the Jonas Brothers and scoring a Billboard 100 hit in 2009, the first ever for a K-pop group. >> Listen to this: "Nobody"

Super Junior
K-pop's "biggest" group has had as many as 13 members over the years. >> Listen to this: "Mr. Simple"

Girls' Generation
The female counterpart to Super Junior, the nine members of Girls' Generation write their own music. >> Listen to this: "Gee"

Big Bang
The so-called "Kings of K-pop," composed of members T.O.P., Taeyang, G-Dragon, Daesung, and Seungri, have found heated competition in BTS. So much so, in fact, that their respective fan groups have stoked a heated rivalry. >> Listen to this: "Bang Bang Bang"

decades gave rise to countless idol groups, to whom BTS owes tribute.

The global shift in the music industry in the information age has been a huge part of K-pop's modern-day success story, which is fueled in large part by the Internet. No artist saw greater proof of that than Psy, whose humorous video for "Gangnam Style" set seemingly unsurpassable records on YouTube, reaching 1 billion views in record time to become the site's most watched video by a huge margin. Six years later, with YouTube the undisputed platform for accessing music videos, it's still the fourth-most-watched video of all time.

Given the established hierarchy in the K-pop industry, BTS's success with an independent label has been shocking—they have long been considered an underdog group since they were recruited under the Big Hit Entertainment umbrella and not by one of the Big Three.

Undoubtedly, the Internet has played a central role in their ascent. Their online popularity is unprecedented, and that has everything to do with their fan base. As *Dazed* magazine put it, "They may still be regarded as an overnight phenomenon by an American media…but even the tiniest peek behind the glittery curtain shows how ferociously BTS have dedicated themselves to nurturing a long-term symbiotic relationship between the group and their fandom."

Their wide-ranging talents, along with the fervency of their ARMY, have taken them to the top of the heap both in South Korea and abroad. And they show no signs of stopping. ◆

4

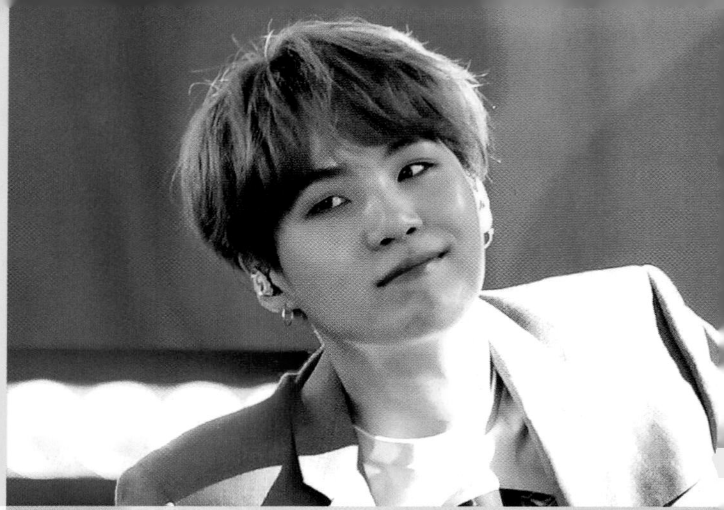

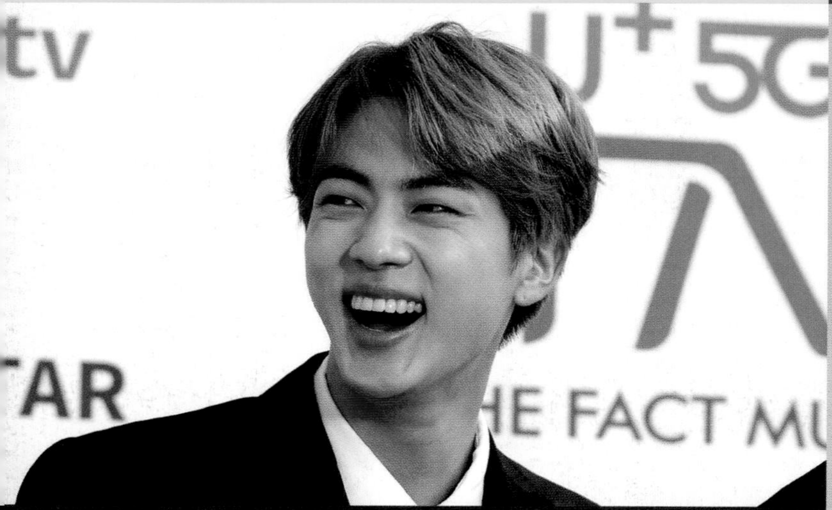

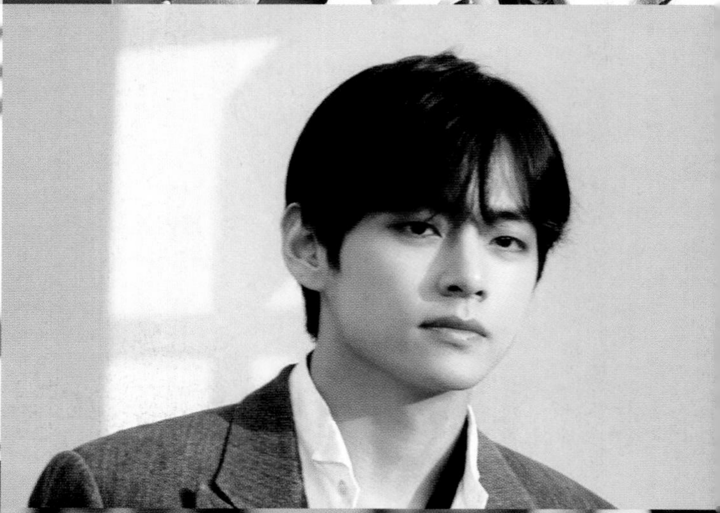

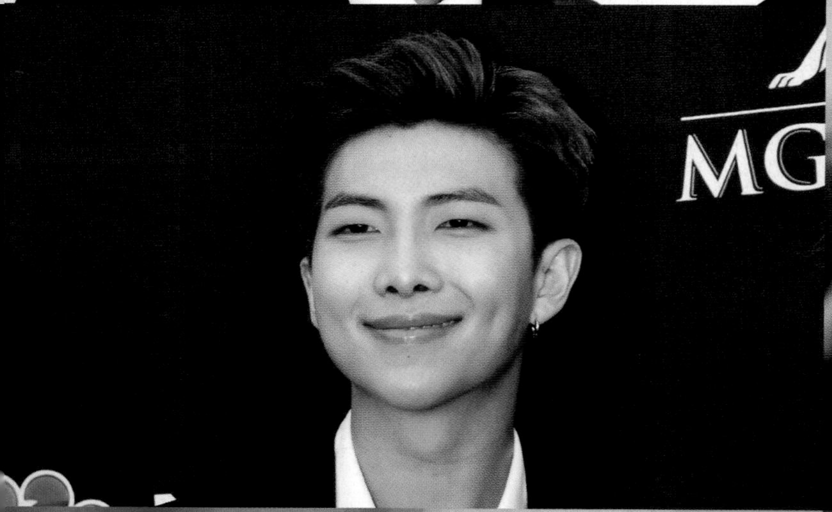

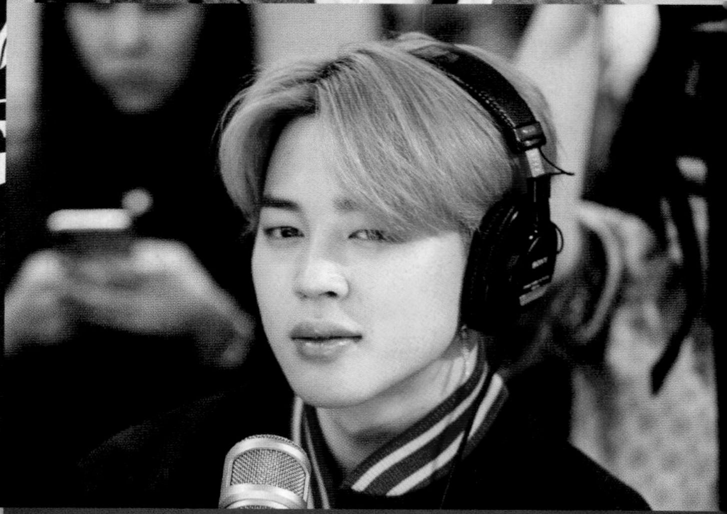

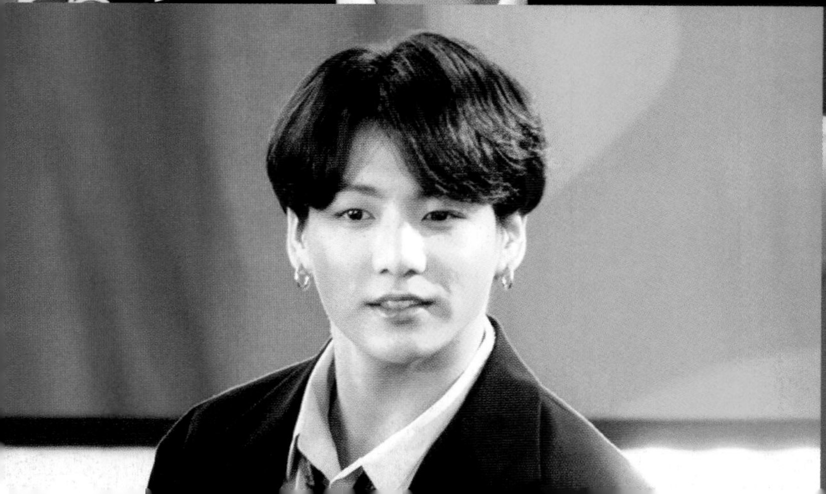

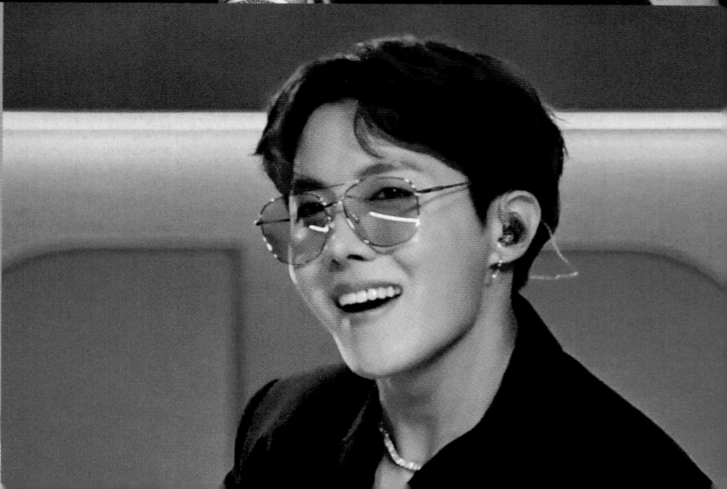

MAKING THE BAND

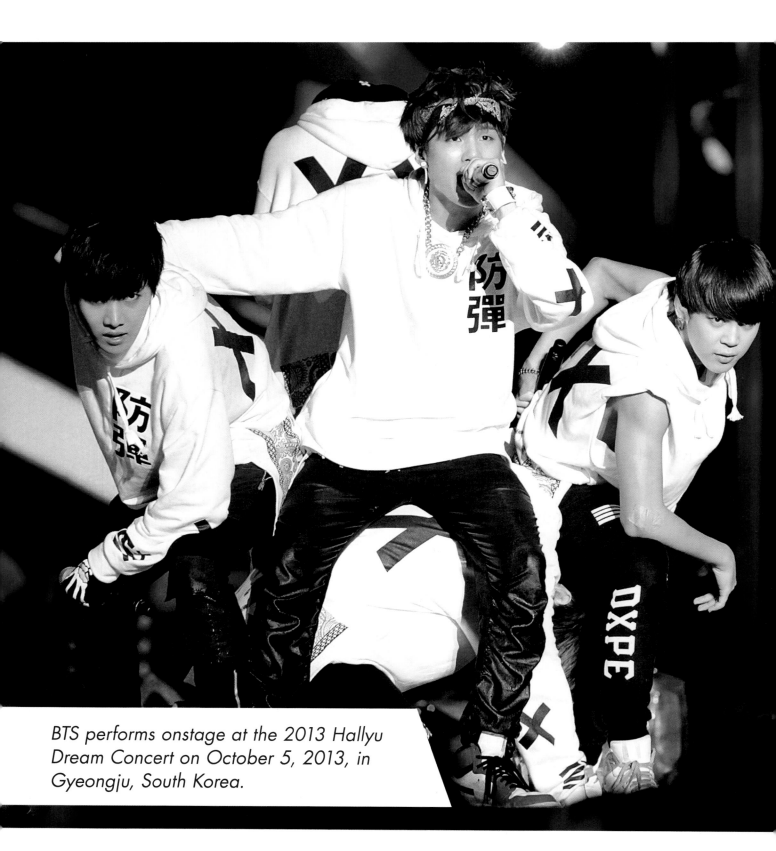

BTS performs onstage at the 2013 Hallyu Dream Concert on October 5, 2013, in Gyeongju, South Korea.

Making the Band

The year was 2010. Big Hit Entertainment was still looking for...well, a big hit. They had a promising recruit in Rap Monster (aka RM), but ultimately Big Hit founder Bang Si-hyuk thought he might fit better into an idol group. Members were scouted through various auditions and brought into the agency's fold as trainees. The roster fluctuated a bit in those early training years, but once Jimin joined in 2013, the ensemble was set: RM, J-Hope, Suga, Jimin, V, Jin, and Jungkook were Bangtan Sonyeondan—translating roughly to the Bulletproof Boy Scouts and better known as BTS.

The members all brought different talents to the table—dancing, rap skills, vocals—but there was one thing that unified them. "All BTS members had self-motivation from their early teenage years," Bang said in a 2013 interview.

"Before joining us, they all struggled despite exceptional enthusiasm in their respective areas of music and dance." Together, the pieces all fell into place.

Bang had risen through the ranks of K-pop, where he saw the formula for making a K-pop success. But the industry was changing. For one thing, the Internet had arrived. In South Korea, the shock waves were severe. "South Korea is one of the most wired countries in the world, and digital piracy devastated its music scene," the *New York Times* reported. "Sales of CDs by units dropped 70.7 percent from 2000 to 2007, according to the International Federation of the Phonographic Industry, the international music industry association."

But as Bang shrewdly recognized, the Internet created opportunity as well. It provided a network for groups to engage with fans directly. And BTS was a presence online long before they made their onstage debut. They launched their YouTube channel, BangtanTV, in 2012, and Big Hit's countdown clock ticked on until June 2013, when Bangtan Sonyeondan made its official debut with the release of their first single, "No More Dream," from the *2 Cool 4 Skool* EP. It was a daring debut that boldly challenged the South Korean establishment. The release earned them a number of Best New Artist awards in South Korea, including Golden Disc Awards and Seoul Music Awards honors.

The band dared to say something, and audiences were listening. Credit that to Bang too, whose initial vision for the group was, well, visionary. Speaking to South Korean newspaper *JoongAng* in 2018, Bang recalled, "I recently came across a company document from the year before BTS debuted, in which we were debating what kind of idol group to create. It said, 'What kind of hero is the youth of today looking for? Not someone who dogmatically preaches from above. Rather, it seems like they need a hero who can lend them a shoulder to lean on, even without speaking a single word.' I didn't want them to be false idols. I wanted to create a BTS that could become a close friend."

what's the WORD?

chincha
Really? As in, "Did you hear that BTS was nominated this year for a Grammy Award?" "*Chincha?* That's awesome!"

WHO am I?

...n you guess the BTS-related celebrity? Following is a list of clues. The fewer clues ...u need to solve the mystery, the better your score. Solving in three or fewer clues is ...ellent and four to seven is good. If you needed eight or more clues, better luck next ...e!

When I was young, I wanted to pursue a career in music; my parents convinced me to attend college instead.

In 2019 Billboard named me one of music's Top 25 Innovators.

I was born in Seoul, South Korea, on August 9, 1972.

I am an award-winning songwriter, but I am better known for my business acumen.

I founded my own company in 2005.

In 2018, Bloomberg calculated my net worth at $770 million.

I am close friends with JYP Entertainment head Park Jin-young, with whom I worked closely for many years.

I have worked with a number of top K-pop artists, from g.o.d. to Rain to the Wonder Girls.

The members of BTS call me by my nickname, Hitman.

. I handpicked the members of BTS and signed them to my label, Big Hit Entertainment.

BANG SI-HYUK

The "father" of BTS, Bang Si-hyuk has found the perfect combination in the group's seven members. It's a testament to BTS's accomplishments that they're seen as Bang's greatest achievement. Bang enjoyed a staggeringly successful music career even before BTS's debut.

College chums with Park Jin-young, he worked as lead music producer for Park's JYP label, churning out hit after hit and in the process earning himself the apropos moniker Hitman. When it came time to spread his wings and start his own venture, he had a different vision for the future of K-pop. He dreamed of an idol group that would connect with everyday youth rather than be a gilded icon for the masses to worship. Relatability, Bang felt, was the wave of the future.

It's abundantly clear that Bang's vision then has come to fruition. It's not just that ARMYs have unprecedented access to their idols; their idols also stand for something. Powerful change-makers and advocates of self-love and acceptance, the men of BTS are one of a kind.

> ## "We started to tell the stories...that other people could not or would not tell." —Bang

If K-pop were all style and no substance, BTS would offer something completely different. "We started to tell the stories that people wanted to hear and were ready to hear, stories that other people could not or would not tell," Suga told *Time* in 2018. "We said what other people were feeling—like pain, anxieties and worries. That was our goal, to create this empathy that people can relate to."

Still, the band wasn't an overnight success. Some viewed the group—who had been groomed as a gritty hip-hop act—to be too harsh and in-your-face. Some felt that the band's extremely confessional lyrics were posturing rather than the real deal. But the band stuck to their guns, making the music—and the message—they wanted. "BTS's climb to success, then, involved the band finding a way to communicate that this confessional image *was* real," Vox.com reported. "They did this by mixing their openness on social media with blunt and honest lyrics—and owning their status as an underdog group battling to succeed against other bands who came from established studios with larger budgets."

The watershed moment came in 2015, when they nabbed their first win on a weekly music show (for "I Need U," on *The Show*). From then on, it all fell into place. Just three years after their debut, BTS had the best-selling album in Korea's history. But they weren't just a Korean

BTS appears at the photo call for their June 15, 2013, debut showcase.

pop QUIZ

A lot goes into choosing the right stage name. Can you identify which member of BTS considered the following names that almost made the cut? (A) Young Kid; (B) Seagull; (C) Gloss; (D) Runcha Randa.

Answers: (A) Jimin; (B) Jungkook; (C) Suga; (D) RM.

smash—they were selling out arenas across the globe.

BTS's international success inarguably goes hand in hand with their ability to use the Internet as a tool. "Bang's focus on fan communications has become the biggest driving force of BTS's popularity," Kwak Young-ho, co-founder of Hanteo Chart, which partners with Billboard on sales data, told Bloomberg. "BTS has now become a platform."

And in turn, the ARMY has been instrumental in spreading the gospel of BTS. "The fandom was able to grow because videos related to BTS were translated into many different languages and posted to sites like YouTube or Twitter in real time," Bang told *JoongAng*.

That fan base continues to grow exponentially. A study conducted by the nonprofit Korea Foundation found that the number of *hallyu* fans has increased by more than 30 million people in just three years. According to *Forbes*, "This drastic increase in the global fandom was largely attributed to the world's biggest boy band, BTS." As BTS continues to spread their message of love, the whole world, it seems, is tuned in. ◆

the BOY BAND formula

When the Beatles arrived in America in 1964, ushering in full-tilt Beatlemania, the Fab Four ignited the country's fascination with boy bands. Since then, bedroom walls have been bedecked with posters of dreamy pop stars who incite their fans to near-riot in concert. But what makes a boy band, anyway? Let's examine the past 50 years of teen idols to answer that question.

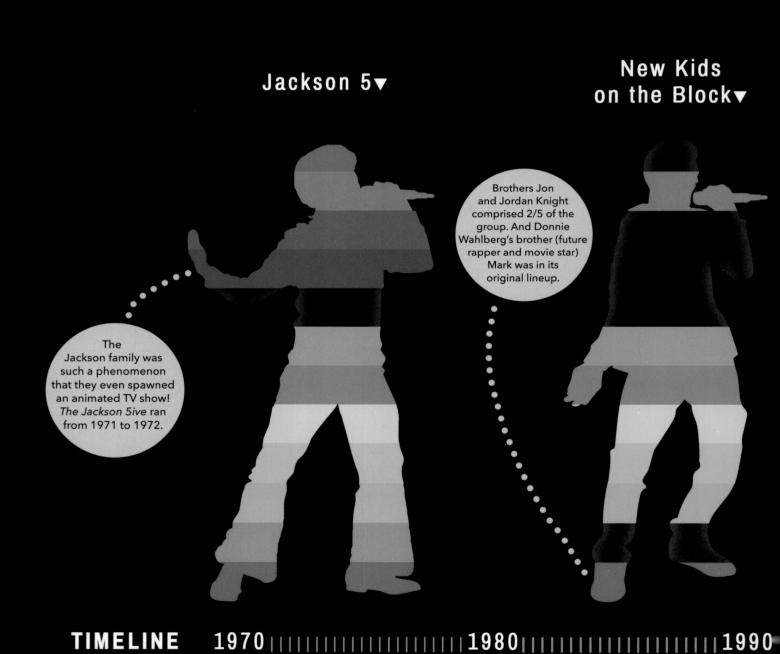

Jackson 5▼

New Kids
on the Block▼

Brothers Jon and Jordan Knight comprised 2/5 of the group. And Donnie Wahlberg's brother (future rapper and movie star) Mark was in its original lineup.

The Jackson family was such a phenomenon that they even spawned an animated TV show! *The Jackson 5ive* ran from 1971 to 1972.

TIMELINE 1970 |||||||||||||||||||||||||| 1980 ||||||||||||||||||||||||||||||| 1990

- SQUEAKY-CLEAN IMAGE
- PRIMARILY FEMALE FAN BASE
- PLAY THEIR OWN INSTRUMENTS
- HAVE A TV CONNECTION
- WRITE THEIR OWN MUSIC
- GREAT HAIR
- MASSIVE MERCHANDISING REVENUE
- RELEASED CHRISTMAS SONG
- SENSE OF HUMOR ABOUT THEMSELVES
- GREAT DANCERS
- MEMBER(S) WENT ON TO SOLO SUCCESS
- FAMILY MEMBERS IN THE BAND

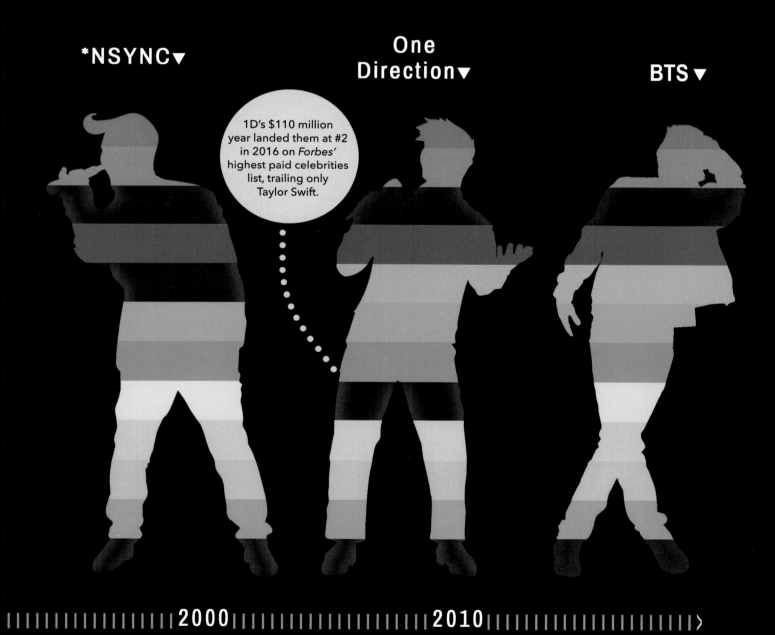

*NSYNC▼

One Direction▼

BTS ▼

1D's $110 million year landed them at #2 in 2016 on *Forbes'* highest paid celebrities list, trailing only Taylor Swift.

2000   2010

5

AN
ARMY
UNITES

BTS has become a global force to be reckoned with because they understand the changing landscape of the music industry—it's all about the Internet. Making inroads in America, streaming sites such as YouTube have made all the difference. Gone are the days of radio play and MTV; in the Internet age, it's all about streaming. "Right now young people both discover and enjoy music on YouTube for free and with great ease—either via laptops or mobiles," reported the *Daily Telegraph*. "It has become both the MTV and CD shop for teenage music-lovers." In fact, according to a recent Nielsen study, nearly two-thirds of U.S. teens say they prefer YouTube ahead of all other music platforms.

This has been a crucial advantage for K-pop, according to experts in the industry, who first saw the genre's views skyrocket from 2 billion to 7 billion in the wake of "Gangnam Style." "It might have been impossible for K-pop to have worldwide popularity without YouTube's global platform," Sun Lee, head of music partnerships for Korea and Greater China at YouTube and Google Play, told

ARMYs camped out in the rain for days inside New York's Central Park in anticipation of BTS's Good Morning America *performance in May 2019.*

BTS takes on the Big Apple, posing for a picture in front of the Empire State Building in 2019. The building was illuminated in purple that same night in honor of the band!

by the NUMBERS

5.2 BILLION. According to YouTube, BTS videos were viewed on the site more than 5.2 billion times in 2018.

Bloomberg. "K-pop is creating a great sensation in the U.S." To date, BTS has eclipsed a staggering 9 billion views across all official YouTube channels.

And it's not just YouTube. Playlists—which three-quarters of online music listeners create, share, or otherwise listen to, and which more than half consider important to their listening experience—have helped introduce BTS to listeners stateside. Spotify reported that streams of Korean music doubled in the first half of 2017, and that listeners in the U.S. made up one-quarter of that audience. (Speaking of Spotify, there you can listen to personalized playlists curated by

each of the Bangtan Boys on their BTS channel.)

All that online buzz has combined to create a fan base that is young, Internet-savvy, and extremely motivated. Consider that, as of this writing, BTS's official Twitter has "only" 16 million followers, yet those followers made BTS the most retweeted Twitter account in 2017—more than Donald Trump and Justin Bieber (with their 62 million and 106 million followers, respectively) combined. They established a Guinness World Record in 2018 as the music act with the most Twitter engagements.

The success comes from their unique brand of K-pop, certainly. But the effect that their fans

what's the WORD?

daesang
Top award. As in, "BTS won their first *daesang* in 2016, nabbing the Melon Music Award for their album *Young Forever.*"

have had on their rise cannot be understated. And for BTS, fan power is a highly utilized resource. Fans are treated to a personal side of their idols and engage with them directly in a way most artists do not. BTS posts around the clock—from candid videos and messages on social media to V LIVE streams to produced content such as YouTube Red's documentary series *BTS: Burn the Stage* and even livestreams of their concerts. If you're following BTS, you know it all.

Their fan base, the ARMY, an acronym for Adorable Representative MC for Youth, has done everything it can possibly do to make sure its idols get their due.

"The BTS ARMY…is the engine powering the phenomenon," reports *Billboard* magazine. "It translates lyrics and Korean media appearances; rallies clicks, views, likes and retweets to get BTS trending on Twitter and YouTube; and overwhelms online polls and competitions. Big Hit says that it makes sure to disseminate news and updates about the band on the fan cafe, so as not to arouse the wrath of the ARMY."

The ARMY was there to hand the band their first win on the prestigious Korean music competition show *Inkigayo* in 2016 by goosing the band's digital sales numbers to help put them over the

Jungkook and Jin give good face during a 2016 performance in Seoul.

Jimin commands the audience's attention at the 2019 BBMAs.

did you KNOW?

BTS is the first K-pop group to have its own Twitter emoji. The social media site created a special emoji for the band: a bulletproof vest emblazoned with the letters BTS befitting the Bulletproof Boy Scouts themselves. Since then, Twitter has added two more BTS-dedicated emojis to the delight of Twitter-pated ARMYs everywhere.

top. They were there again when the band simultaneously hit No. 1 on all eight of the Korean charts (an "all-kill") with "Blood Sweat & Tears." And they were there to elevate the band's album sales and YouTube views to levels never before seen by a Korean idol group.

In the U.S., BTS *owns* Billboard's Social 50 chart. They've been at No. 1 for the better part of three years at last tally. The band also took home the Billboard Music Award for Top Social Artist in 2017, becoming the first Korean artist ever to win a BBMA. They won again in 2018, with even more ARMYs in attendance to celebrate. (BBMA host Kelly Clarkson wore noise-canceling headphones when she introduced them for their onstage performance.)

They hit *Time*'s Top 25 Most Influential People on the Internet list in 2017. And when the magazine reached out to readers to ask who should be included in its annual Time 100 list, the ARMY was there too. They made BTS the No. 1 vote-getter, by a margin almost 10 times more than the closest competitor. It's little wonder that they're considered South Korea's No. 1 Power Celebrity, according to *Forbes*. As industry analyst Jason Joven put it, "The BTS ARMY,

BTS Sets Multiple Guinness World Records

"Idol"

It's no secret that the ARMY is a formidable force, and one of the most influential fan bases in pop music today. And it's because of the ARMY that BTS has obliterated some of the most unreachable milestones in music and social media, making them a bona fide worldwide phenomenon and earning them inclusion in the definitive volume of records itself: originally *The Guinness Book of Records*, later *The Guinness Book of World Records*, and now titled simply *Guinness World Records*.

The Guinness Book of Records was a book borne of necessity. Sir Hugh Beaver, then managing director of the Guinness brewery, conceived of the idea as a tool to settle the ordinary pub argument. Which bird flies the fastest? What's the longest road in the world? What's the tallest building? A preliminary list of superlatives was compiled and published in 1955. In the years that have followed, the list of accomplishments has grown and grown—including many that Sir Beaver never could have conceived.

BTS set several Guinness benchmarks for Twitter engagement, the most notable among them becoming the most retweeted Twitter user of all time. And most recently, the music video for "Boy with Luv" broke three YouTube records, including most viewed YouTube video in a 24-hour period. (And they did that by breaking their own record—with 74.6 million views of "Boy with Luv" eclipsing their 45 million views on the day "Idol" was released.)

empowered by their freedom from close-minded stereotypes of Asian artists and a diligent mastery of digital coordination, simply brings fandom to another level."

That immensity is not lost on the band, who constantly thank their fans for their support and inspiration. "I…attribute the glory to all of our ARMYs," Jin told *Billboard* after the band hit the Hot 100 for the first time. "I think that even if you make music, you need people to listen to it in order to climb up. I'm always grateful to ARMYs and love them." It's gratitude they echo time and again.

BTS has captured the hearts and minds of people around the world, and celebrities are not immune to the fever. The band's fans in Hollywood include: Emma Stone, Jimmy Fallon, Ansel Elgort, Terry Crews, *Game of Thrones*'s Maisie Williams, Demi Lovato, Perez

Hilton, Wale, Charli XCX, Camila Cabello, Charlie Puth, Major Lazer, James Corden, Zedd, Jared Leto, Shawn Mendes, Tyra Banks, Laura Marano, DNCE, Marshmello, Ellen DeGeneres, Khalid, and John Cena, among many others.

ARMYs continually demonstrate their devotion to their chosen idol group, but what's often overlooked is their devotion to one another. It's not unusual to see ARMYs standing up for one another or sending each other messages of encouragement or kinship. They truly are a family unto themselves, and a globally connected community of disparate personalities.

Bringing people together is indeed one of the greatest achievements BTS has had so far in their still-blossoming career. Across the generations and the miles, they have cultivated a fan base that embraces not only love for the band but for one another. The West Coast fan group U.S. BTS ARMY typifies this ethos, writing that their mission statement is "to inspire, celebrate and spread BTS's message of love and acceptance to ARMYs and any others who cross [their] path."

When BuzzFeed published a story that interviewed black BTS fans who had experienced racism within the fandom via the social network Curious Cat, the ARMY mobilized. Twitter user and BTS fan @cultfye rallied fellow fans, creating the hashtag #blackARMYsmatter and shutting it down. The hashtag went viral, and the responses were powerful. "You're not an army if you're racist, we don't accept racism in this fandom and we never will," @KJCOSMOS tweeted. "For all ARMYs: speak up for black armys or poc [people of color] when you see things like this happening. It shouldn't be happening. Help be

the solution, not the problem." BTS fans may not have invented the idea of the support group within a fan group, but they appear to have perfected it.

Incidents of negativity are few and far between within the fandom. You won't find many trolls lurking among BTS's 16 million followers. BTS's Twitter page is a veritable oasis in the online realm, where negativity is often the stock in trade. Instead, with BTS, it's a total love-fest.

"I am amazed by ARMYs power to do good every day. One Tata sticker [led] someone to share their story, talking about issues that many face. It's a pay forward come to life and all because of @BTS_twt's positive influence," wrote @lsglr. It's impossible to underscore. ◆

J-Hope gives love to the crowd during a 2017 performance on Jimmy Kimmel Live.

can't stop, WON'T STOP

May 4–5, 2019
Rose Bowl, Los Angeles, CA

May 11–12, 2019
Soldier Field, Chicago, IL

May 18–19, 2019
MetLife Stadium, East
Rutherford, NJ

May 25–26, 2019
Allianz Parque, São Paolo

If BTS has an insane connection with their fan base, one of the main reasons must be because they spend so much time up close and personal with the ARMY. In April 2019 they wrapped their Love Yourself tour, which crisscrossed Asia, Europe, and North America—including 15 sold-out U.S. dates. Not content to rest, BTS announced their encore, their international Love Yourself Speak Yourself world tour,

June 1–2, 2019
Wembley Stadium, London

June 7–8, 2019
Stade de France, Paris

July 6–7, 2019
Yanmar Stadium Nagai, Osaka

July 13–14, 2019
Shizuoka Stadium Ecopa,
Shizuoka

which began in May 2019. The first round of dates has them again performing for audiences around the globe, and to no one's surprise, they've been selling out shows as fast as tickets have gone on sale. Maybe you're one of the lucky ones to catch a performance by your idol. If not, stay tuned. Their comeback tour can't be too long in the making. (That's K-pop speak for next musical release.)

THE
MAGNIFICENT
SEVEN

BTS takes New York! Performing during the Love Yourself Speak Yourself tour in Newark, New Jersey.

The Magnificent Seven

I mean, sure, the ARMY loves all things BTS—the music, the message, the slick videos, the killer choreography. But we can't forget the band's most important asset—well, seven most important, actually. For the uninitiated, consider this your formal introduction.

J-HOPE

"Hope is always near us, so be brave!"

J-Hope is the band's pocketful of sunshine, the playful member who always seems to have a ready smile for his bandmates and his fans. It's fitting, then, that he's the middle member of the band in age, and he describes himself as the link between the older age line (Jin, RM, and Suga) and the younger (Jimin, V, and Jungkook). The unofficial "mood-maker," he's the one who lifts the other guys' spirits. As leader RM puts it, "If I'm fire, J-Hope is water. He's good at 'turning off' my bad habits. He's really sociable, so he's good at mixing with others and our group members."

J-Hope began as a street dancer in his native Gwangju and achieved award-winning success as a competitive dancer. Ultimately, this led to his recruitment by Big Hit and his inclusion in BTS, where he serves as the lead dancer for the band. Initially slated to be one of the singers, he became the third addition to the band's rap line instead.

He released his long-gestating mixtape, *Hope World*, in March 2018. (With only hours of eligibility before the week's album sales closed, *Hope World* not only cracked the Billboard 200 but became the highest-ever charting

fun FACT

When wrestler John Cena posted a picture of J-Hope on his Instagram, ARMYs the world round wondered whether he was a BTS stan with a Hobi bias. Since then, his fandom has been confirmed, full-stop. "J-Hope is my favorite...because he's got a little bit of street cred, like myself," he told *Entertainment Tonight* in 2018.

by the BOOK

J-Hope's *Hope World* draws its inspiration from the 1870 Jules Verne adventure classic *Twenty Thousand Leagues Under the Sea* (and J-Hope plays the lyrical role of its hero, Captain Nemo) and nods to Douglas Adams's *The Hitchhiker's Guide to the Galaxy*, among other allusions. J-Hope often uses literary references in his songwriting. Little wonder, considering he is the son of a literature teacher.

K-pop solo act in the chart's history.) Inspired by RM and Suga's efforts to release solo mixtapes, he wrote and produced the personal and reflective seven-song album. "I started dancing first, but felt I could also tell my story through my music," he told *Time*. It confronts some of the same issues that BTS tackles in its own music, including the trappings of fame and struggles to find inner peace. Unsurprisingly, like its creator, *Hope World* oozes with positivity and whimsy.

Like the rest of his bandmates, he considers BTS's success to be a privilege but also a great responsibility. His goal is to keep writing and creating for the ARMY. Speaking to *Elle* in 2017, he said, "The music helped me sympathize with our young generation and also empathize with them. I'd like to create and write more music that represents them."

VITAL stats

Name: Jung Ho-seok

Hometown: Gwangju

Birth Date: February 18, 1994

Musical Birthday Twins: The infamous Yoko Ono (1933), dancing icon John Travolta (1954), and hip-hop king Dr. Dre (1965)

Nicknames: Hobi, Sunshine

Childhood Dream: To be a "normal" college student

Musical Influences/Dream Collaborators: Becky G, Benzino, A$AP Rocky

Hobbies/Interests: Shopping; movies, especially melodrama; collecting toys

Known For: Infectious positivity, fastidiousness

Bad Habits: Fidgeting

Favorite Color: Green

Favorite Food: All Korean food, especially kimchi

Favorite Number: 7

Pet Peeves/Dislikes: Messiness

Phobias: Everything from snakes to bugs to roller coasters to horror movies…the list goes on

Motto: "If you don't work hard, there won't be good results."

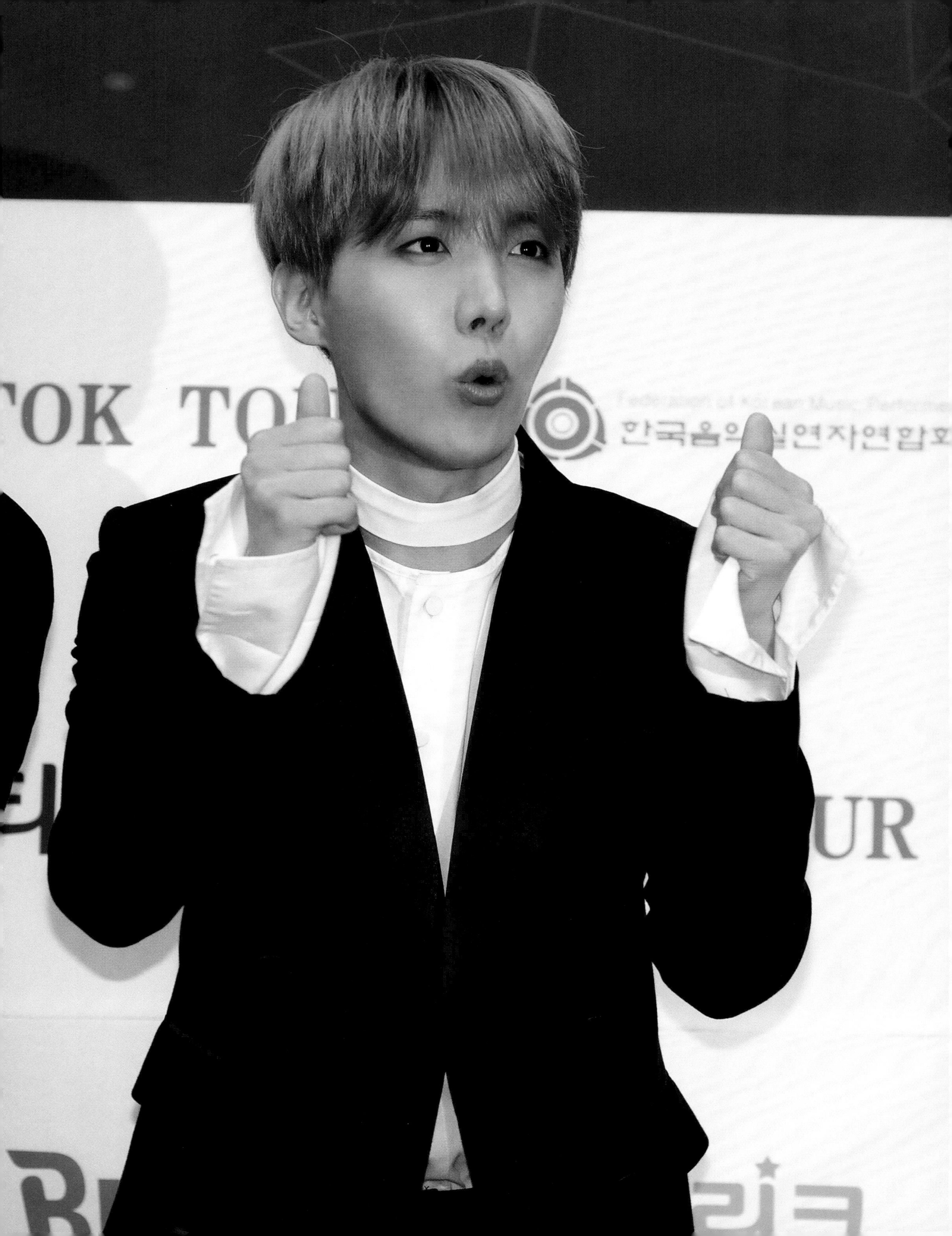

JIMIN

"No matter how hard it is right now, think of what the result will make you feel."

The man, the myth, the abs. Besides being just a pretty face, Jimin is one of the band's vocalists and dancers, the man "with the jams" and the irrepressible swag.

He is also arguably the emotional core of BTS. Whenever one of the members is struggling, Jimin seems to be there with a helping hand or a word of encouragement. (The guys unanimously agree that he's the one to go to when they need to relieve stress or need comfort or warmth.) He is empathic and openhearted, trustworthy, and loyal.

ARMYs often relate to his vulnerabilities, including his struggles with bullying and his appearance. He has been particularly candid about his past battles with his weight. That vulnerability is evidenced in his craft, too. When asked by *Elle* magazine what message he wanted fans to receive from BTS's music, he said, "It would be really great if our

fun FACT

Jimin's stage name was almost Baby J or Young Kid, but in the end he decided to go with his given name.

all the right MOVES

You can see it onstage—Jimin's dance moves are crisp, precise, and yet fluid. That's thanks in part to his background as a dancer. Before joining Big Hit, Jimin attended Busan High School of Arts, where he studied modern dance. It was a high school teacher who encouraged him to pursue a K-pop tryout (to the delight of millions of fans, of course).

music continues to touch people. Once your heart is moved, it will develop to something better and positive."

Jimin released his first solo song, "Promise," in 2018. Listeners streamed it more than 1.4 million times on SoundCloud in the first hour of its release!

He's a hard worker who's extremely tough on himself, and he doesn't take failure lightly. He practices his dancing exhaustively. Jimin has said that the one thing he can't live without is eyeliner, even in practice sessions. According to him, it's the magic ingredient in projecting *aegyo* and strong expressions through dancing. He often says that his best feature is his eyes.

As bandmate J-Hope put it in an interview with *Exile* magazine, "Jimin…was born with cuteness. Another thing is that although he is younger than me, he sometimes has the attitude of a *hyung*. So I think that's his charm."

With his infectious laugh and incredible vocal range, he's an indispensable member of the group, which he considers a second family. And his warm, gooey center has won over many an ARMY.

VITAL stats

Name: Park Ji-min

Hometown: Busan

Birth Date: October 13, 1995

Musical Birthday Twins: The incomparable Paul Simon (1941) and soulstress Ashanti (1980)

Nicknames: Chimchim, Dolly, Ddochi ("puppy"), Jiminie

Childhood Dream: To become a policeman

Musical Influences/Dream Collaborators: Troye Sivan, Big Bang, Rain, Wiz Khalifa

Hobbies/Interests: Movies, comic books, exercise

Known For: Insane work ethic (he's the one who pushes the other guys to practice when they don't want to), his eye smile, his abs

Bad Habits: Incessantly forwarding things on social media

Favorite Color: Light blue

Favorite Food: Meat

Favorite Number: 3

Pet Peeves/Dislikes: Being teased about his voice or weight

Phobias: He's afraid of butterflies, and has been since someone pranked him by putting one in his underwear (yikes!)

Motto: "Don't let go of something that makes you a better person."

JIN

"When something is delicious, it's zero calories."

Jin is the band's official "visual" and the so-called handsomest member of the group. But it turns out that the moniker Worldwide Handsome is actually self-invented. "I gave myself [the name] 'Worldwide Handsome.' It's a nickname that I came up with during an interview," he told *Billboard* magazine. "Even I find it a little embarrassing to say, but many people like it, although I'm not actually worldwide handsome. Ever since our debut, I've been calling myself good-looking. You could think of it as a kind of rote teaching." In part, Jin's "handsome" image is a deflection. Turns out he's a little bit insecure, like all of us. We seldom see him wearing his glasses, even though he has a strong prescription. He is also self-conscious of his hands; he has a condition called swan neck deformity that makes his fingers curve like, well, a swan's neck.

One of the group's singers, his honey-coated vocals absolutely slay on BTS's ballads. He has a

fun FACT

Jin loves video games and rarely goes a day without gaming. His fellow bandmates say that there's no better way to annoy him than to hide his Nintendo.

eat, Jin, EAT!

Jin's "Eat Jin" videos are the stuff of legend. Jin loves eating so much that he says no matter how tired he is, there are two words that will always get him going: "Let's eat!" Jin loves trying out new recipes, using his bandmates as guinea pigs. If he wasn't in BTS, he says he'd be a cooking show host. A delicious idea!

certain way of making fans feel he's performing only for them. He is quite possibly the most natural of the group at *aegyo* (flirting); you'll often see him winking and blowing kisses at the camera. Even Tyra Banks, the high priestess of the smize, has complimented Jin on his perfect eye smile.

Jin himself admits to being a less-than-natural dancer, but you'd never know it seeing him onstage. He's confident and charismatic, and he works extra hard to make sure his moves are as crisp as his bandmates'.

Despite being the eldest of the group, Jin is often kidded for being the band's most childish member (a unanimous consensus among the guys). Blame that on his silly sense of humor. When he's not spoiling the Bangtans with delicious suppers, he's doing silly dances or making "dad jokes." Jin's energy and enthusiasm lift the band up when they're down, in addition to motivating them on a day when they're fatigured. Suga calls his *hyung* a "human energy drink."

Jin is many fans' bias because he's not afraid to show his feminine side, because of his cheesy sense of humor, and yes, because of his strikingly handsome face!

VITAL stats

Name: Kim Seok-jin

Hometown: Gwacheon

Birth Date: December 4, 1992

Musical Birthday Twins: Beach Boys founder and musical genius Dennis Wilson (1944) and hip-hop legend Jay-Z (1969)

Nicknames: Worldwide Handsome, Observant Jin, Shoulder Hyung (for his broad shoulders, natch)

Childhood Dream: To become a detective

Musical Influences/Dream Collaborators: The Chainsmokers (again)

Hobbies/Interests: Cooking, photography, collecting toys

Known For: Cleanliness, culinary prowess (he once made J-Hope cry tears of joy over a bowl of seaweed soup)

Bad Habits: Snoring

Favorite Color: No more Pink Princess; Jin says his favorite color is now blue

Favorite Food: Lobster, cold noodles, and basically any and all fried food

Favorite Number: 4

Pet Peeves/Dislikes: Skipping meals

Phobias: Scary movies

Motto: "Let's live freely."

JUNGKOOK

"Let's get it!"

Jungkook may be the *maknae* (youngest) of the group, but he is no less hardworking than his bandmates. A triple threat—singer, dancer, and rapper (check out his flow on "No More Dream")—Jungkook is a tireless worker who preaches the philosophy "Effort makes you. You will regret someday if you don't do your best now." And if you think that's just lip service, consider what he told *Yonhap News* in 2018: "I came to think that this year I need to do things that will help my career as a singer so I plan to quit gaming and focus on three things: I want

to ace in playing the piano, foreign language, and singing." For those who know Kookie, that's pretty major indeed!

fun FACT

Jungkook is probably the most athletic member of the bunch—he's a natural at everything from fishing to archery and everything in between—and motivates his *hyungs* to hit the gym. His bandmates even gave him the nickname Jeon Cena—a nod to ARMY (and former WWE superstar John Cena)—in honor of his wrestling prowess.

talent upon TALENT!

Jungkook is interested in all things photography, and has lately turned an eye toward directing. "With still images, people have to look at it and then translate what they're looking at, but videos are moving so people can translate what the video is right away," Jungkook told *Entertainment Weekly*. "That's why I like video."

As the band's youngest member, he often reflects on how he came of age as a member of the band. To him, they are a second family, and each one of them has influenced who he has become as a man. It is a brotherhood for which he is eternally grateful. "The guys filled me in one by one. They put the scattered pieces of my puzzle back together," he said in *BTS: Burn the Stage*.

But it's not all serious reflection with Jungkook. He's probably the band's biggest prankster, and perhaps the quickest to get the guys to laugh. A certified goofball, he's also a voracious consumer of contemporary music, with influences as wide-ranging as G-Dragon (his ultimate idol) and Dutch duo DROELOE to Troye Sivan and Billie Eilish.

He's a little brother to all his *hyungs*, which means he sometimes gets teased by the other members but also manages to get away with a little bit more too (hence the nickname Devil Maknae). His cutie-pie looks, bottomless talent well (artistic and athletic?!), and velvety-smooth voice have won ARMYs the world over.

VITAL stats

Name: Jeon Jung-kook

Hometown: Busan

Birth Date: September 1, 1997

Musical Birthday Twins: Crossover pop star Gloria Estefan (1957), multihyphenate Zendaya (1996)

Nicknames: Jeon Junkookie, Golden Maknae, International Playboy, Devil Maknae

Childhood Dream: Becoming a restaurant owner or tattoo artist

Musical Influences/Dream Collaborators: Billie Eilish, Big Bang's G-Dragon, Macklemore, Justin Bieber, Charlie Puth

Hobbies/Interests: Drawing, video games, exercise

Known For: Crazy drawing ability, bunny smile, *aegyo*

Bad Habits: Sniffling (he has rhinitis), untidiness

Favorite Colors: Red, black, and white

Favorite Food: Pizza, bread

Favorite Number: 1

Pet Peeves/Dislikes: When older fans call him *oppa* ("big brother"). "All of my ARMY, from now on bring your identification cards," he once quipped. Word to the wise, he'd rather be called *aegi* ("baby") than *oppa*!

Phobia: Microwaves and big bugs

Motto: "Living without passion is like being dead."

RM

"You can't live without love."

The leader of the group and its first member, RM (formerly Rap Monster), started out as an underground rapper, making a name for himself in the scene around Seoul. Big Hit saw a star in Rap Monster, and he joined their ranks in 2010. Over the next three years, the agency put together the magic combination that would become BTS.

RM is known for his introspection, intelligence (he reportedly has a 148 IQ!), and charisma. He is the driving force for the group, charging them with the responsibility of being more than just an idol group. In the YouTube series *BTS: Burn the Stage*, he talks about going beyond connecting with fans who just think of them as cute or their music as catchy: "We want to listen to their stories. We want to look into their eyes and see what lives they lead and become a

fun FACT

RM taught himself English by watching the American TV show *Friends*. His parents bought him the complete series on DVD, and he studiously watched them—first with Korean subtitles, then with English subtitles, and finally with no subtitles at all.

no more MONSTERS

Until 2017, Kim Nam-joon went by the moniker Rap Monster. Now known as RM, he said he changed it because the name was seen by many as too forceful. However, he also dropped a tantalizing tidbit for ARMYs at a press call in 2017: "I don't plan to restrict myself to rapping in the future, and I didn't want to come off as too aggressive, which is why I thought about changing my name."

part of the lives of those who love us so that we can be a big help to them."

RM has led the charge in this endeavor, writing some of the band's most powerful songs, from their debut "No More Dream" (about the cookie-cutter expectations placed upon teenagers) to "21st Century Girl" (addressing women's rights) to "Spine Breaker" (taking on consumerism) to his solo offerings, such as the heartbreaking "Forever Rain." He is also one of the band's most political members, who boldly breaks the idol mold to speak out about issues that concern him.

RM also speaks impeccable English. All of these things make him the natural spokesperson for the group in the U.S. When asked why K-pop is finally making waves in America, he revealed the secret of BTS's success, as well as their core mission: "The world is getting smaller and smaller, and we're one of the groups that has most benefited from the new media. And music is a universal language. Thanks to fans, they're always translating our lyrics and messages…. This is the right time for K-pop [in America]."

Judging by their success so far, he may indeed be right.

VITAL stats

Name: Kim Nam-joon

Hometown: Seoul

Birth Date: September 12, 1994

Musical Birthday Twins: Seductive soulster Barry White (1944), country music legend George Jones (1931), and music competition royalty Jennifer Hudson (1981)

Nicknames: Dance Prodigy (on account of his clumsy dancing), RapMon, God of Destruction

Childhood Dream: Becoming a security guard

Musical Influences/Dream Collaborators: Pharrell Williams, Lil Nas X, Drake, Eminem

Hobbies/Interests: Computers, reading, collecting toys

Known For: His prodigious and socially conscious songwriting, work ethic, dimples

Bad Habits: He tends to lose or break things easily (Suga said he "should stay in his room for the world's peace.")

Favorite Color: Black

Favorite Food: Korean knife noodles

Favorite Number: 1

Pet Peeves/Dislikes: Tight pants, when people blast music nearby

Phobias: Self-doubt

Motto: "This too shall pass."

SUGA

"We wanted to use our abilities and skills and…inspirations to help the world."

Suga may be sweet, but he actually got his name because of his looks—specifically, his pale complexion and, according to Big Hit impresario Bang Si-hyuk, his sweet smile. The man who jokingly (or not-so-jokingly?) calls himself a genius is one of its three rappers, and its unanimous "swag master." (He's definitely got swag—and a sense of humor. When asked what his go-to pickup line is, he quipped, "Do you know BTS?" Aces!)

"Suga. Genius." Like Jin's handsomeness, it's a self-dubbed title that also happens to be true. He began his musical journey as a classical musician before turning his eye to a career in K-pop. But as he

told *Elle* magazine in 2017, he has always been a writer. "I have [been] writing rhymes and lyrics, a habit since I was a kid. They are all the little minor feelings and thoughts

fun FACT

A classically trained musician, Suga decided to change course and pursue a career in pop music after hearing Korean reggae star Stony Skunk's "Ragga Muffin" in sixth grade.

"first LOVE"

For the uninitiated, the "love" in the Suga-penned "First Love" is actually not a person at all but the piano. He even accompanied himself on the piano while performing the rap onstage during the Wings tour.

that go through my mind. I shuffle them a year or so later, and they sometimes become great lyrics for songs." That practice seems to have paid off, as Suga has created some of the best and most brutally honest verses in all of BTS's catalog.

He has written frankly in his lyrics about his struggles with depression and also on his very personal mixtape *Agust D*. ("I've denied my nature many times / My address is idol and I won't deny / The anguish that dug into my mind countless times," he writes on "The Last.") His transparency is something that has resonated deeply with fans, many of whom credit BTS with helping them through difficult times. The

ARMY considers itself a support group unto itself, and the boys of BTS, especially Suga and RM, have helped bring some difficult issues—especially those people are less likely to verbalize—to the forefront.

Maybe it's his ice-cold stare, his rapper's growl, his lyrical prowess, his songwriting and producing prowess, or the smile that could melt glaciers that makes him his fans' bias. Whatever the reason, he's an integral member of the band, and one who's helped separate BTS from the pack of idol groups through his candid and fearless songwriting.

VITAL stats

Name: Min Yoongi

Hometown: Daegu

Birth Date: March 9, 1993

Musical Birthday Twins: Jazz legend Ornette Coleman (1930) and rappers Chingy (1980) and Bow Wow (1987)

Nicknames: Motionless Min (because he likes to be lazy on off-days), Agust D

Childhood Dream: Becoming an architect or concert pianist

Musical Influences/Dream Collaborators: Drake, Kanye West, Lupe Fiasco, Lil Wayne

Hobbies/Interests: Photography, basketball

Known For: Nonstop songwriting, sleeping in

Bad Habits: Nail-biting

Favorite Color: White and black

Favorite Food: "Meat, meat, meat."

Favorite Numbers: 3, 93

Pet Peeves/Dislikes: Crowds and noise (maybe he's in the wrong business?)

Phobias: Loud noises, such as fireworks

Motto: "Let's live while having fun."

V

"I have a big heart full of love, so please take it all."

Known for his killer stare, powerful voice, and bottomless bandana collection, V is the second-youngest member of the group and its wackiest. His "4-D" personality constantly bemuses his bandmates. As RM once quipped, V is "10 percent genius and 90 percent idiot."

He's also BTS's unofficial social butterfly, boasting a large number of famous friends in the industry, including musicians and actors from Park Bo-gum to Park Seo-joon and Kim Min-jae. He's also a talented actor in his own right. In 2016–17, he starred in the K-drama *Hwarang*, where he won acclaim for his role as the playful but troubled young poet-warrior Suk Han-sung. His bandmates agree that he's the best actor among them, and could have a career in K-drama if he wanted. (He wouldn't be the first to graduate from the K-pop ranks to the silver screen.)

His goofy and dramatic side is well-known, but he also has a flip side. His bandmates tease him about his Blank Tae moniker, but being stone-faced isn't a total invention. Just check out BTS's appearance on *The Late Late Show with James Corden*. The band tried

fun FACT

V first coined the phrase "I purple you," which means "I love and trust you unconditionally." Purple is the most trusted of the colors, he said, as it is always at the bottom of the rainbow, holding up the rest of the colors. So *that's* why their socials are littered with purple hearts. *Jjang!*

state of V ART

Jungkook may be the one in the band most associated with art—and his drawing talent is killer—but V just so happens to be an art connoisseur. When asked what his favorite things about touring America were, he answered emphatically: the Museum of Modern Art in New York and the Art Institute of Chicago. Whenever time allows, he likes to stop at museums when on the road.

their hand at the show's popular segment "Flinch" (in which guests stand behind a Plexiglas wall while objects are hurled at them with great speed). Not only did V not flinch; he didn't even move.

He also has a tender side and is dedicated to ARMYs, especially young children. You'll often find him stopping for autographs and taking photos with his youngest fans. Sweet, sensitive, and impossibly sassy, V is many fans' bias, and an integral member of the group. (K-drama will have to wait!)

VITAL stats

Name: Kim Tae-hyung

Hometown: Daegu

Birth Date: December 30, 1995

Musical Birthday Twins: Classical-pop mash-up mastermind Jeff Lynne (1947), pop princess Ellie Goulding (1986), and made-for-TV Monkees bandmates Mike Nesmith (1942) and Davy Jones (1945)

Nicknames: TaeTae, CVG (because his moves are perfect like a computer video game character), Blank Tae (on account of his blank expression), Gucci Boy

Childhood Dream: Becoming a professional saxophonist

Musical Influences/Dream Collaborators: Coldplay, Post Malone, Maroon 5, Lauv, Childish Gambino

Hobbies/Interests: Animation, shopping

Known For: Eccentricities (Koreans call it "4-D")

Bad Habits: Nail-biting, yells and kicks in his sleep

Favorite Colors: Black, white, and green

Favorite Food: Japchae (a Korean stir-fried glass noodle dish)

Favorite Number: 10

Pet Peeves/Dislikes: Wearing shoes

Phobia: He's afraid of heights too

Motto: "Forget what hurt you but never forget what it taught you."

BEHIND THE MUSIC

From the jump, BTS's music made a statement. Their bold first single, "No More Dream," sent shock waves through the K-pop ranks, heralding a musical act that was a force to be reckoned with. More specifically, they had a point of view, and they weren't afraid to take on topics that are considered taboo in Korean society and elsewhere.

Challenging the status quo is a primary focus—BTS wants to be nothing less than a change agent. The group's leader articulated why they felt the responsibility to verbalize some of the struggles facing today's young people. "Honestly, from our standpoint, every day is stressful for our

The seven members of BTS are a spectacular combination.

generation. It's hard to get a job, it's harder to attend college now more than ever," RM told *Billboard* magazine. "Adults need to create policies that can facilitate that overall social change. Right now, the privileged class, the upper class needs to change the way they think." Suga picked up the thought: "And this isn't just Korea, but the rest of the world. The reason why our music resonates with people around the world who are in their teens, twenties, and thirties is because of these issues."

BTS's wide-ranging scope doesn't only extend to politics. They are highly influenced by art, history, and especially literature. (A brief tour of their music videos reveals a treasure trove of influences as disparate as writers Ursula K. Le Guin and Robert Louis Stevenson, Dutch painter Bruegel, and Greek mythology.) "We try to make our

own BTS context," RM told *Billboard* magazine. "Maybe it's risky to bring some inspiration from novels from so long ago, but I think it paid off more. It comes through like a gift box for our fans. That's something you can't find easily from American artists."

Beyond the scope of the lyrics, BTS has striven to experiment with and expand their sound. The group's seven members bring with them a multitude of strengths and musical influences, and together their music touches on hip-hop, EDM, classical, R&B, and everything in between. They've amassed a huge amount of material already…and they show no signs of stopping anytime soon.

The following discography charts BTS's releases so far, not including their three full-length Japanese-language releases—*Wake Up*, *Youth*, and *Face Yourself*—and eight Japanese EPs. ◆

The album that started it all. Upon its release, Big Hit heralded the effort as "a fresh new take on '90s hip-hop" and "a new, bold message…'What is your dream?'" In its album review, SeoulBeats.com gave a surprisingly prescient conclusion, writing, "BTS could be en route to unveiling something fantastic."

2 Cool 4 Skool
Released June 13, 2013

inside the TRACK

2. "We Are Bulletproof Pt. 2"

This anthemic single serves as a rallying cry for the Bulletproof Boy Scouts, whose fan base quickly adopted "ARMY" as an extension of the metaphor.

inside the TRACK

4. "No More Dream"

Their very first single, it addresses the anxieties of living up to parents' expectations. Vox.com calls it an "ode to teen apathy."

O!RUL8,2?
Released September 11, 2013

inside the TRACK

2. "N.O."

Another paean to adolescent malaise, the "N.O." in this case stands for "no offense."

inside the TRACK

6. "Coffee"

"A remake of Urban Zakapa's 'Café Latte,' BTS reworked the 2009 song to fit their own distinct vibe. With smooth raps and rock strings spurring along the original jazz melody, 'Coffee' is as equally crestfallen lyrically as the original but has a more playful tone that fits the youthful feel of the septet's *Skool* era," *Billboard* reported.

BTS continued to stretch the boundaries of K-pop with songs such as "N.O.," which push back at the societal expectations put upon young people. "You can't be trapped in someone else's dreams," the lyrics urge. Two months after the album's release, BTS won their first major award: Best New Artist at South Korea's Melon Music Awards. (They'd also win the same honors at the Gaon Chart Music Awards, Golden Disc Awards, and Melon Music Awards that same awards season.)

With *Skool Luv Affair*, they earned their first No. 1 nomination on a weekly music show on *Inkigayo* for "Boy with Luv," another breakthrough moment.

Skool Luv Affair
February 12, 2014

inside the TRACK

2. "Boy in Luv"

"Propulsive with its rock and hip-pop sound, 'Boy in Luv' switched things up for BTS stylistically," *Billboard* reported, "shifting away from the aggressive tone and contentious themes of their first year's releases in favor of an enthusiastic ode to young love. The group lives up to their boyish name with this single."

inside the TRACK

5. "Just One Day"

This single was a major turning point for the band, "the first time the group slowed down a bit and put the dulcet quality of their vocalists front and center," *Billboard* observed.

Dark & Wild
Released August 19, 2014

Their first full-length album, *Dark & Wild* explores the themes of love and loss. The album cover is even emblazoned with the warning: LOVE HURTS, IT CAUSES ANGER, JEALOUSY, OBSESSION, WHY DON'T U LOVE ME BACK? "The fact that BTS has only been a presence in K-Pop for a year is almost inconceivable," reported Kpopstarz.com in its review of the album. "*Dark & Wild* is an album which showcases the best aspects of Korean music while providing the opportunity to reach global audiences with a unique sound."

inside the TRACK

6. "Rain"

No relation to the K-pop titan of the same name. "Written in part by the rap-line, the lyrics to 'Rain' detail gloomy slice-of-life scenes that are overcast with worries," reported *Billboard*. "The empty space between the clipped piano notes adds a jazzy flair to the hip-hop sample. 'Rain' proves BTS are adept at painting moods with swatches of gray weather."

inside the TRACK

11. "24/7 = Heaven"

"There may be people who say that 'love stories aren't hip-hop,' but we put it in because we believe that it's an important keyword for those in their 10s and 20s," said Rap Monster in 2014.

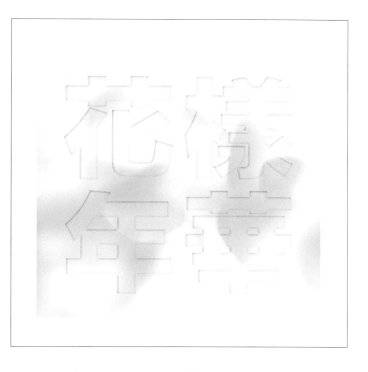

The Most Beautiful Moment in Life Pt. 1
April 29, 2015

inside the TRACK

2. "I Need U"

The boys think this is the best of their songs to listen to when you're sad. "When you're sad, you need to listen to a sadder song," Jin told Buzzfeed.

"The Most Beautiful Moment in Life Part 1 was both the clearest distillation of BTS's sound to date and their most varied offering. They pull each style off with aplomb, giving the various genres their own distinct spin and, thematically, delivering 2015's most accomplished K-Pop album," reported *Pon De Way Way Way.* The first entry in the *Most Beautiful Moment in Life* cycle, it won top honors at South Korea's Golden Disc Awards. It also hit radar screens across the pond; in June 2015 Fuse TV called it one of the best albums of the year so far.

inside the TRACK

5. "Dope"

Shot in one take, the music video for "Dope" is pure spectacle, chock-full of mind-boggling choreography and pitch-perfect routines. It is required viewing for all new fans.

The Most Beautiful Moment in Life Pt. 2
November 30, 2015

inside the TRACK

2. "Run"

Discussing the second installment of their *Most Beautiful Moment in Life* cycle before its release, the band said, "Part one explained how youth is tiring and difficult, and it also touched on how we feel like we're always on edge. Part two will have a more adventurous and daring feel to it. That's why our title song is 'Run.'"

Seven months after *The Most Beautiful Moment in Life Pt. 1*, BTS returned with their comeback in *Pt. 2*, which became their best-selling album to date. Eight tracks charted on Billboard's World Digital Songs chart, another best for the group. As *Billboard* noted in its review, the record contains "some of the most honest performance[s] the group has created to date…. It's [the] key, empathetic moments that prove BTS has something that makes them very clearly stand out from other new boy bands."

This combined issue includes remix versions of *MBMIL* songs and also features three brand-new tracks: "Fire," "Save Me," and "Young Forever."

The Most Beautiful Moment in Life: Young Forever
May 20, 2016

inside the TRACK

6. "Silver Spoon"

This track tackles the socioeconomic hierarchy of South Korea head-on. The "spoon" one is born with (golden, dirty, etc.) signifies one's station in life. It expresses the anxiety of the younger generations and what their predecessors have left them, and pushes back at the near-constant expectation that they work ever harder to achieve success. "Stop going on about 'effort' and more 'effort' / It makes my skin crawl," goes the refrain. *Billboard* calls it "one of BTS's most impactful songs."

WINGS

Wings
Released October 10, 2016

inside the TRACK

2. "Blood Sweat & Tears"

"Blood Sweat & Tears" was the group's first single to achieve an all-kill, hitting No. 1 on all eight Korean charts simultaneously.

inside the TRACK

8. "MAMA"

Americans are familiar with the English-language meaning of "mama," but it also stands for Mnet Asian Music Awards, a top prize in South Korea. For the better part of two decades, the Big Three had a stranglehold on the prize, until BTS broke through in 2016. A tribute to parental support during the lean times, could the boys have also had the MAMAs in mind?

Perhaps the only album of 2016 inspired by a Hermann Hesse novel, *Wings* is an ambitious and bold offering that tackles such universal themes as temptation, loss, and growth. Fuse TV raved about the album, announcing, "By [letting] each dude shine on a song completely separate from the others, the guys have the chance to explore their own personal creativity while still going strong with the group's brand identity. That is arguably the most important part for all of their careers to ensure they're *all* in the industry for a long time to come."

By the time BTS released the first of their *Love Yourself* albums, the group was regarded stateside as a K-pop outfit that could have real longevity. They also began to get widespread media attention, from everyone from talk show hosts to mainstream music critics. "Ease is the most striking aspect of *Love Yourself: Her*," the *New York Times* wrote in its review. "Each rapper showcases a different approach: Rap Monster with bluster, Suga with slick talk and J-Hope with tricky double-time rhymes. But there's no sense of muscling for turf—just the easy swagger of artists who know they're in control."

Love Yourself: Her
September 18, 2017

inside the TRACK

2. "DNA"

More than just a pop banger, "DNA" was the band's first entry into the Billboard Hot 100. The music video, awash in kaleidoscopic colors, is also the band's most viewed— with more than 764 million views as of this writing.

inside the TRACK

8. "Go, Go"

"It isn't a BTS album if there isn't a track criticizing society," Suga said of this song, which explores the emptiness of materialism.

With the second of the *Love Yourself* albums, BTS reached a giant milestone, debuting at No. 1 on the U.S. album charts. It received widespread acclaim from ARMYs and media alike. "*Love Yourself: Tear* is K-pop with genre-hopping panache," reported *Rolling Stone*. "Throughout it all, the members of BTS affect melodic sincerity, singing with intensity and melisma, rapping in tones that show their effort and strain, as if caring never went out of style."

Love Yourself: Tear
Released May 18, 2018

inside the TRACK

2. "Fake Love"

BTS's highest-charting single to date, it made *Rolling Stone's* list of the top 50 songs of 2018. "Guitars sulk and kick like Eighties Def Leppard, while the blocky bass lines are tenacious enough to compete with Atlanta hip-hop; brusque rapping tugs against intricate, swooping singing," the magazine wrote.

inside the TRACK

7. "Magic Shop"

Jungkook got his first production credit for this song, which pays tribute to ARMYs everywhere.

WHO am I?

you guess the BTS-related celebrity? Following is a list of clues. The fewer clues
need to solve the mystery, the better your score. Solving in three or fewer clues is
llent and four to seven is good. If you needed eight or more clues, better luck next

am a Grammy-nominated artist.

was born on November 30, 1977.

My father is a famous restaurateur.

am of Japanese descent.

hold three Guinness World Records: most traveled musician in a single year and,
or the same show, longest crowd cheer and most glow sticks used in a 30-second
span.

have worked with many recording artists, everyone from Kid Cudi and Drake to
Louis Tomlinson and Linkin Park.

My albums include *Neon Future*, *Neon Future II*,
Neon Future III, and *Neon Future IV*.

A lot of people recognize me by my signature
ong hair and beard.

am a music producer, songwriter, and record
abel head, but I am best known for my DJing
skills.

am the man who produced BTS's first
Billboard Top 40 hit.

STEVE AOKI

DJ and producer Steve Aoki has been instrumental in breaking BTS in America. His 2017 remix of "Mic Drop," featuring Desiigner, helped the Bangtan Boys nab their first Billboard Hot 100 entry and the band's first No. 1 spot on the iTunes singles chart. It also became the band's first single to be certified gold by the RIAA. BTS returned the favor, handing Aoki his own Billboard Hot 100 single in "Waste It on Me" in 2018.

It turns out Aoki and BTS are a mutual admiration society. "These guys are geniuses," Aoki told *Billboard*.

Suga calls Aoki "an amazing older brother. And his passion for music was one of his many qualities that I respect," *Billboard* reported in a separate interview.

Aoki also sees BTS as arbiters of a far greater achievement than just musical success. "When I was a teenager, one Asian face really stood out: Bruce Lee," Aoki told *Rolling Stone*. "I wondered why there were no other Asian people out there. Now you have seven guys from Korea…that are representing [Asians in the U.S.] in this way that hasn't really been felt at that level of power and influence."

"They're bigger than music. It's cultural; something really powerful for Asian people around the world," Aoki told *Metro UK*. "I see them as something much larger than just the songs they make. I'm excited and honored to be able to work with them."

Answer combines songs from the previous *Love Yourself* albums and includes seven new tracks. *Billboard* called it "a masterwork," and *Clash* magazine wrote, "With so many records previously broken, this new release was one with high expectations attached, and this masterful compilation, which perfectly pays homage to previous releases and simultaneously moves the journey of BTS into a new era, stands out as [the] magnum opus from a group that is ready to scale new heights."

Love Yourself: Answer
Released September 8, 2018

inside the TRACK

1. "Euphoria"
Jungkook's solo song is the perfect anthem for self-love, setting the stage for the album that follows. The production also demonstrates the boundaries that BTS continues to test; the Grammy Museum described it as "an art-pop rabbit hole looking to the future."

inside the TRACK

15. "Idol"
"Idol" brims with bravado, especially with strong verses from the rap line. But the message is as ebullient as any in the *LY* cycle. "You can't stop me loving myself," Jimin intones in the chorus.

MAP OF THE SOUL PERSONA

Map of the Soul: Persona dropped in the spring of 2019 to enthusiastic reviews from fans and critics alike. Even *Pitchfork* couldn't hate on BTS's latest effort, writing, "The rappers—RM (or Rap Monster), J-Hope, and Suga—anchor the group, not only keeping it moored to a unified aesthetic amid constant stylistic shifts but dictating much of what happens in the music…. BTS seem more poised and more in sync than ever."

Map of the Soul: Persona
Released April 12, 2019

inside the TRACK

2. "Boy with Luv"

That catchy hook makes this the perfect radio single—*oh my my my*, it's impossible not to sing along. The collaboration with Halsey became their highest-charting single to date, and their performance at the BBMAs was hands down the highlight of the night.

inside the TRACK

4. "Make It Right"

Ed Sheeran cowrote this song, which found its legs on the Billboard Hot 100 and remains a fan favorite on the record.

BTS promotes Map of the Soul: Persona *on* "iHeartRadio Live with BTS" *at iHeartRadio Theater in New York on May 21, 2019.*

10
MOMENTS
THAT MADE
BTS

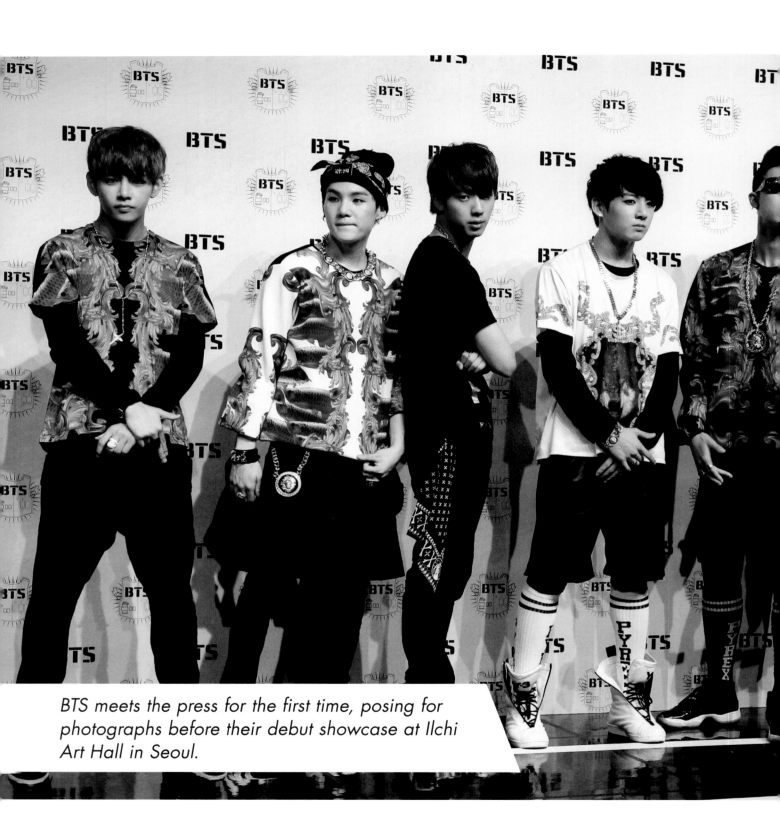

BTS meets the press for the first time, posing for photographs before their debut showcase at Ilchi Art Hall in Seoul.

June 15, 2013
BTS Makes Their Big Debut

The culmination of years of training, preparation, and behind-the-scenes effort finally paid off when Big Hit premiered its idol group, Bangtan Sonyeondan—the Bulletproof Boy Scouts—for music industry insiders and media in Seoul. The band was on hand to showcase its *2 Cool 4 Skool* album, performing the lead single "No More Dream" and "We Are Bulletproof Pt. 2." The album, which features a grittier hip-hop flavor than latter-day BTS offerings, still features familiar BTS hallmarks, especially in its social commentary.

"BTS has repeatedly said that hip-hop is genuine music for telling one's story," Big Hit announced, "and indeed the members rap about their own experiences and emotions. There is no discontinuity between the emotions and lyrics of BTS." ARMYs can agree that that statement is as true of BTS then as it is today.

November 13, 2013

BTS Wins Best New Artist at the Melon Music Awards

Just five months after the debut of their first single, "No More Dream," BTS won their first major award—Best New Artist at South Korea's Melon Music Awards.

The Melon Music Awards are one of the top four most prestigious awards in South Korea, alongside the MNET Awards, Golden Disc Awards, and the Seoul Music Awards. Melon, in particular, factors online sales and fan support—and in this case it was an early indicator of the power of the ARMY.

Several more awards would follow for the Bulletproof Boy Scouts in the subsequent months, but it was the Melon award that first put them on the map for fans in their native country.

BTS takes the stage to accept Best New Artist honors at the Melon Music Awards in 2013.

Members of BTS greet fans at the 2014 KCON in Los Angeles.

August 10, 2014

BTS Has First Scheduled Appearance for U.S. Audiences at KCON

Their first U.S. performance has now been relegated to a footnote, but true ARMYs know that their first gig was actually at the Troubadour in Los Angeles. (The band gave a surprise performance at the venerable club in the midst of filming the Korean reality series *American Hustle Life* with American hip-hop artists Warren G and Coolio, among others.) But their first-ever scheduled performance was at the convention KCON, which has been a huge launching pad for K-pop artists stateside. There, the Bangtan Boys appeared alongside industry giants including Girls' Generation and G-Dragon, among many others. (They went on to headline KCON in 2016.)

In its coverage of the convention, *Billboard* reported, "Rookie boy band BTS might have been the newest artist on the bill, but the huge crowd reaction could have made you think otherwise."

Since its inception in 2013, KCON has expanded to multiple locations in the U.S. and around the world, bringing audiences a taste of the full *hallyu* experience, spanning music, movies, and television. It is the preeminent forum for fans of K-pop—and *hallyu* culture at large—to get up close and personal with their idols. And for BTS, it was their first chance to be face-to-face with American ARMYs.

May 5, 2015

BTS Wins First No. 1 Spot on South Korean Music Competition Show

It was a long time coming, but on May 5, 2015, BTS finally nabbed top honors when they performed "I Need U" on the weekly competition show *The Show*. Finally winning *The Show* was a coup for BTS—an "underdog" from outside the Big Three system—who would go on to win many more weekly titles thereafter.

Weekly television competitions are a huge indicator of a K-pop band's success, and are among the most watched television programs in South Korea. There are six major music shows in the country, one of which airs each day from Tuesday until Sunday: respectively, SBS's *Inkigayo*, MBC's *Show! Music Core*, KBS's *Music Bank*, Mnet's *M Countdown*, MBC Music's *Show Champion,* and SBS MTV's *The Show*. Furthermore, each show has its own criteria for determining its winner.

The shows are a platform for acts to promote their newest music, but more importantly they solidify idols' fan groups. "Korean music show awards tap into the gratification factor for fans who vote daily," *Billboard* reported. "The presence of a physical trophy and encore stage adds a viscerally satisfying element to fan and idol efforts to land the No. 1 spot on the music show charts."

BTS's first win proved to be a major milestone indeed, boosting album sales of *The Most Beautiful Moment in Life Pt. 1* and solidifying their standing as a K-pop force to be reckoned with.

BTS gives an early performance on a South Korean weekly competition show, MBC's Show Champion, on October 9, 2013.

Fans react to BTS on the red carpet at KCON 2016 in Newark, New Jersey.

October 29, 2016

BTS Tops Billboard's Social 50 Chart for the First Time

Today it's no secret that BTS's meteoric rise to fame has been fueled by the unparalleled Internet engagement of their fans. But back in 2016 it was a shock to music industry insiders and fans alike when they became the social media kings of music, stealing the throne from the likes of mainstays Justin Bieber, Selena Gomez, and Ariana Grande.

Addressing the audience after winning Top Social Artist in 2017, an incredulous RM said, "I still cannot believe that we're standing here onstage at the Billboard Music Awards—oh my God."

Since then, BTS has enjoyed an effective stranglehold on the Social 50. As of this writing, they have spent 132 weeks at the top of that chart—they won their third straight Top Social Artist award at the BBMAs in April 2019—and there has been no credible threat to their dominance.

May 21, 2017

BTS Appears at the Billboard Music Awards, Wins Top Social Artist

It was a coming-out party for BTS, no stranger to ARMYs but largely unknown to American audiences. Even *Vogue* took notice, naming the group, dressed in bespoke suits by Anthony Vaccarello for Saint Laurent, the best-dressed artist of the night. BTS also took home the honors for Top Social Artist—a feat they would repeat in 2018 and 2019.

Billboard was an early champion of BTS in the American market, and offered fans some of the group's earliest press coverage stateside. It's fitting, then, that BTS would mark a number of firsts with Billboard: its first major U.S. award, its first major awards performance

(at the 2018 BBMAs, a year later), and the Top Group or Duo prize at the 2019 ceremony.

Additionally, the group has also had major traction on the Billboard charts, especially the Social 50. What's more, they've had three albums debut at No. 1 on the Billboard charts, seven singles rank on the Hot 100, and the band has reigned at No. 1 of the Artists 100 chart, a cross-platform chart that, according to Billboard, "measures artist activity across key metrics of music consumption, blending album and track sales, radio airplay, streaming and social media fan interaction to provide a weekly multi-dimensional ranking of artist popularity."

BTS's first appearance at the BBMAs was a rousing success. The band accepted an award for Top Social Artist and fans turned out en masse to welcome their idols to the U.S.

Flying high at the 2017 AMAs.

November 17, 2017

BTS Performs "DNA" at the American Music Awards

Mark it down as yet another first. When BTS took the stage at the 2017 AMAs, they were the first-ever K-pop act to perform at a major American music awards show. And, performing their song "DNA," they brought. Down. The. House.

Friend and superfan Ansel Elgort was in the front row, cheering on his buddies with unabashed zeal. Audience members including Jared Leto, the Chainsmokers, and Miley Cyrus were wowed too—along with millions of viewers at home. It was a coming-out party for the band, who earned loads of new fans overnight. (In fact, *Good Morning America* reported that there had been *20 million tweets* about the band's blockbuster AMA performance overnight.)

But what was also immediately obvious was that the ARMY was already in the house. Reporting on the performance, *Spin* noted, "With complex choreography that incorporated rapid fire footwork and an on-the-nose double helix formation, the group of 20-to-24-year-olds bowled over the many adoring fans shown on TV who mouthed along to the song's lyrics and attempted to mimic the intricate choreography." The ARMYs' fan chants were definite and deafening, blending with the song in perfect synchronicity.

In short, it was the perfect introduction to the full BTS concert experience—brought straight to your living room.

June 2, 2018
**Love Yourself: Tear
Debuts at No. 1 on the
Billboard 200**

It was breaking news when *Love Yourself: Tear* hit the top of the Billboard chart. Not only did it vastly exceed industry predictions but it became the first-ever offering by a K-pop act to hit the top of the charts. (In fact, only one other K-pop album had ever cracked the top 10—their own *Love Yourself: Her*, seven months earlier.)

ARMYs were quick to rejoice. The group even received a stunning congratulatory message from South Korean president Moon Jae-in, who tweeted: "The songs, dance, dreams and enthusiasm of BTS energized and gave strength to young people around the world."

"At the very heart of BTS's outstanding dancing and singing is sincerity," Moon continued. "This magical power turns grief into hope and differences into similarity. Each of the seven members sings in a way that is true to himself and the life he wants to live. Their melody and lyrics transcend regional borders, language, culture, and institutions.

"*Bangtan*, which literally means bulletproof in Korean, was born out of the will to protect teenagers from prejudice and oppression. The names of each member— Jin, Suga, J-Hope, RM, Jimin, V and Jungkook—are going to be remembered for a long time. Thank you to BTS for spreading joy across Korea and the world with your great performances."

BTS performs onstage during the 2018 Billboard Music Awards.

BTS performs during an appearance on Saturday Night Live.

April 13, 2019
BTS Plays *Saturday Night Live*

Breaking yet another huge barrier, BTS became the first-ever K-pop act to perform on the series. The iconic sketch comedy show, in its 44th season, is one of comedy's gold standards. But it has also given audiences its fair share of landmark musical performances. Over the years the program has played host to everyone who's anyone in the music industry.

Getting onto the *SNL* stage is a feat unto itself. The eyes of an international audience are on you, good or bad. (Just ask Ashlee Simpson, whose recording career effectively ended after she was caught lip-syncing on the live broadcast.) For their parts, BTS did themselves and K-pop proud, staging their intricately choreographed performances of "Boy with Luv" and "Mic Drop" on a vastly smaller stage at NBC's Studio 8H.

The reaction by ARMYs was massive, as expected. But it also gave the band a wider television audience. "Every generation gets its own crop of boy bands, but BTS feels like an unusually potent force," NPR reported in its review of the band's *SNL* performance. "Its sound seems to straddle the whole world, the songs are catchy as anything and each member brings enormous charisma to the mix. Lots of bands can seem strangely diminished by the *SNL* stage on TV, but on Saturday night, BTS filled every inch of the frame with flashy motion— tight choreography, bright colors, bold energy."

In its quest for world domination, BTS took yet another huge step forward on *Saturday Night Live*.

April 21, 2019

BTS Performs Hat Trick, Capturing Third Straight No. 1 Album

With the debut of *Map of the Soul: Persona*, BTS proved once and for all that they're a force to be reckoned with. The album took the top spot on the charts, selling 230,000 units in its first week. What's more, it was the band's third No. 1 album *in less than a year's time*. If that doesn't sound impressive, consider that the last group to achieve that feat was another so-called boy band named the Beatles. (Heard of *them*?)

In fact, BTS's sales figures just keep climbing. Consider that *Love Yourself: Tear*, which hit No. 1 in May 2018, sold 135,000 units in its first week. *Love Yourself: Answer* sold 185,000. The sky seems to be the limit for BTS, as the ARMY grows ever stronger.

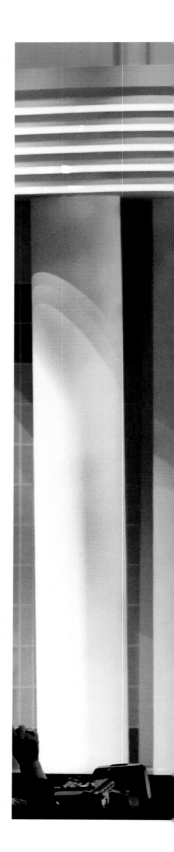

BTS performs "Boy with Luv" from Map of the Soul: Persona at the 2019 Billboard Music Awards.

DOLLARS
AND
SENSE

Members pose with the Palisade, the new flagship sport utility vehicle from Hyundai Motor Company. The band is the promotional envoy for the Palisade global brand.

Dollars and Sense

Since their debut in 2013, BTS has released 14 Korean-language albums as well as 3 full-length albums and 8 EPs in Japanese. It's an incredible output for any musical act, much less one that spends so much of its time on tour. It's obviously a testament to the indefatigable work ethic of BTS. It also translates to a massive amount of earnings.

Their success has helped Big Hit Entertainment grow exponentially, thanks to its biggest-profile artist, BTS. The once-fledgling label doubled its profits between 2017 and 2018, overtaking all Big Three labels in net profit—a once-unthinkable feat.

BTS is also a promotional juggernaut. They are the face of some of the biggest companies in Korea, including Hyundai and Samsung, and also have endorsement deals with Puma (for which they are global ambassadors), LG Electronics, Lotte Duty Free, SK Telecom, VT Cosmetics, KB Kookmin Bank, Dunkin' Donuts, and Coca-Cola, among others. Not only is the group a recognizable face with an unimpeachable

what's the WORD?

Q score
A valuable tool for advertisers, it quantifies an individual or group's familiarity and favorability.

Q score, but they also have a social media reach that is untouchable. When BTS announced its partnership with LG on a new line of smartphones, LG announced that its social media channel was "flooded" by more than 1 million visitors. The company also described itself as an underdog in taking on cell giants Samsung and Apple, much like BTS and Big Hit have taken on the Big Three. It's a compelling story that has translated into big sales.

"Thanks to BTS, foreign fans flock to online markets to purchase K-pop merchandise," Moon Ji-young, head of Global Affairs at eBay Korea, said. The *Korea Times* reported that there are almost 40,000 BTS-related items for sale on the site. Their merchandising reach is vast. There are BTS figurines, video games, apps, and merch, merch, merch. Everything from apparel to backpacks to jewelry… even BTS-branded facial masks for fans to wear during cold and flu season (or on a trip to South Korea, where the air quality is notoriously bad). Even Mattel is getting in on the game, releasing a line of hotly anticipated BTS dolls, replete with the band's colorful outfits from the "Idol" music video.

In-concert sales are also massive. Consider that practically everyone in the crowd performs Army Bombs with an official BTS light stick. (Don't know what that is? Check out the impressive displays on YouTube.)

Hey BTS
Want to get you
new BTS do

SCAN TH
PRE-ORDER

#BTSxMatte

Mattel's BTS dolls make their own debut.

And in another shrewd marketing move, BTS is opening up a pop-up store for their merch in various tour stops during the Love Yourself Speak Yourself run. The stores in Chicago, New York, London, Paris, and Los Angeles will be open for one week, and will carry exclusive merchandise that will not be available online or at concert venues.

"They're so creative on every level—on their dance, on their sound, on their style, their flow, creatively musically,

creatively on the fashion tip," frequent collaborator Steve Aoki told *Billboard*. "They're brand developers. They developed their own brand, and they're global."

BTS has also capitalized in markets that have yet to be lucrative or proven. Their first concert film, *Burn the Stage: The Movie*, earned $18.5 million to become the highest-grossing event cinema of all time (beating bygone boy band phenoms One Direction). Their second concert film, *Love Yourself in Seoul*, broke further records,

nice CRIB!

BTS is movin' on up! In 2018 they moved to perhaps the most exclusive residence in Seoul—the apartments at Hannam the Hill in the Hannam-dong district near Mount Namsan. The address is home to some of the most famous celebrities and socialites in Korea, and affords its residents with strict privacy. And how are the digs? Luxe! One apartment in the building sold for $7.5 million. The move is a natural result of BTS's success, no doubt, but it's important to note that even now, the band members choose to live under the same roof.

WHO am I?

Can you guess the BTS-related celebrity? Following is a list of clues. The fewer clues you need to solve the mystery, the better your score. Solving in three or fewer clues is excellent and four to seven is good. If you needed eight or more clues, better luck next time!

1. I was born on September 29, 1994.

2. I adopted my stage name from the name of a New York City subway stop.

3. I can play several musical instruments, including the violin, cello, viola, and guitar.

4. Like my future collaborator Justin Bieber, I leveraged my YouTube success into a record deal.

5. I have collaborated with a wide variety of musicians, including Khalid, Big Sean, Sia, and (of course) BTS.

6. I am known for speaking my mind about some really controversial subjects as well as my own past.

7. I have two No. 1 Billboard hits: my single "Without Me" and the Chainsmokers' "Closer," on which I featured.

8. My real name is Ashley Nicolette Frangipane.

9. Performing with BTS was my first-ever time dancing choreographed steps in a music video.

10. My collaboration with BTS is the band's highest-charting single as of this writing.

HALSEY

BTS and Halsey met at the 2017 Billboard Music Awards and quickly struck up a friendship. "I just met BTS and they are the coolest! WOW," Halsey tweeted from the event. Flash forward two years, to their epic team-up, "Boy with Luv." The single debuted in Billboard's top 10, becoming the highest-charting single for a K-pop act ever. And its pastel-drenched music video (which Halsey describes as "my pink dream with my pink friends") surpassed YouTube records to become the site's most watched video in a 24-hour span.

Despite the language barrier, which Halsey dismisses as "unimportant," they've forged an unshakable bond. "We have been friends for almost 2 years! I am so lucky to know them and they inspire me so much. your boys are A+," Halsey tweeted to ARMYs everywhere.

RM called Halsey BTS's "eighth member" in an interview with *Extra*, and the "octet" put on a blockbuster performance of "Boy with Luv" live at the Billboard Music Awards in 2019.

The band's Coke ad, which ran during the 2018 World Cup and through the summer.

becoming the largest event cinema release of all time, playing in 3,800 theaters across 95 countries, *Forbes* reported. Their third concert film, *Bring the Soul: The Movie*, landed in August 2019.

In June 2019 BTS livestreamed their concert from Wembley Stadium on the V LIVE streaming app. Fans around the world were able to watch their idols up close and personal, for the bargain price of $28 a pop. It's a natural progression for BTS, who have proven themselves time and again to be on the forefront of the changing musical landscape.

It's clear that the demand for anything and everything BTS is enormous, but what is less often discussed is their massive ripple effect on the music industry and the Korean economy at large. Consider that BTS is the official ambassador for tourism in South Korea—and not just in name only. According to a study done by the Hyundai Research Institute, BTS was responsible for bringing 1 of 13 South Korean tourists to the country in 2017—800,000 people! In short, they're a seven-man *hallyu* wave bringing in a staggering $3.6 billion a year in revenue to their home country.

But that's not all. The Institute also reported that an additional $1 billion in consumer exports related to BTS were sold overseas. Should BTS's popularity continue, they are expected to generate $37 billion in revenue over the next decade. (And considering BTS's still-growing popularity, that number could get much, much bigger.) It's an unprecedented accomplishment, no doubt, and it underscores Korea's commitment to its entertainment industry. It is indeed big business. ♦

Celebrating the opening of tourist attraction K-Star Road in 2015.

how BIG is BTS?

The members of BTS are bringing in an eye-popping $3.6 billion in revenue to South Korea annually. But what does that actually amount to? We ran the numbers to give you a little perspective on how that stacks up. With $3.6 billion...

...you could equal the net worth of Steven Spielberg, filmmaker and producer with more than five decades of blockbusters under his belt and who ranks No. 2 on *Forbes'* list of richest celebrities.

...you could purchase 130,434 Ford F-Series trucks, the best-selling automobile in the U.S.

...you could buy 11 McDonald's cheeseburgers for every person in the U.S.

...you'd be just shy of the combined gross domestic product of the U.S. and British Virgin Islands.

10

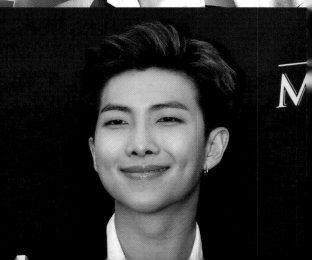

SPEAK YOURSELF

The secret of BTS's success is a combination of factors, from their understanding and mastery of how an artist can use social media to their socially conscious music to their individuality in personality and style.

"K-pop isn't taking over the world; BTS is," reported *Dazed* magazine. "Their unique vision for art and music is singularly queer, fluid and androgynous in ways that no other boy band is achieving on the same global scale. Because of this, their existence itself is political, and they embrace that by speaking up for issues young people face. Of all the meaningful things they've said over their career, the quote that encapsulates them perfectly is the statement of simple acceptance that opens each of their concerts. RM always says a variation on this: 'Please be mindful of each other;

your neighbors, your friends, your lovers, or whoever.'"

BTS "[switches] seamlessly between what is considered feminine and what is considered masculine in a way that is thrilling—and liberating," reported the *Daily Vox*. "Their tremendous global platform provides them with a means of creating a new norm for masculinity, one that is more organic and experimental." They can rock tailored tuxedoes as easily as they do pink hair and eyeliner—sometimes simultaneously.

Being themselves is something BTS does unapologetically, from displaying vulnerability in their songwriting to their challenging of the Western and Asian masculine archetypes. They simply refuse to be categorized or defined by someone else.

Not only has BTS been included on *Time*'s Most Influential list for

BTS's lyrics are a call to action, and one of the many ways in which they speak themselves.

three years straight, but perhaps more important, they've also been named one of the magazine's Next Generation Leaders. Leading by example is a mission they take to heart every day, and their message of self-love and acceptance has resonated with those who hear it. They acknowledge their flaws and talents in equal measure.

BTS consistently uses their music as a vehicle for activism. The *Skool* albums tackled the hardships and expectations faced by adolescents, and the *Love Yourself* cycle centered around the theme of self-acceptance.

As *Affinity* magazine reported, "They channel powerful emotions into upbeat and seemingly happy songs, transforming them into symbols of this generation's battles. This ability to amplify so many voices on such a large scale, and in mainstream worldwide media, is

what leads to the powerful sense of community that their fanbase (dubbed ARMY) shares—they're not only supporting artists, but they're also working *together* to create positive change. Combined with the rare sincerity and openness of the group, BTS's music and actions have encouraged fans to apply the same values in their own lives and contribute to a better and kinder environment."

And that better and kinder environment isn't just about how ARMYs treat each other. It's about what they're doing for the world at large. Rather than sending gifts to the band, BTS encourages charitable donations. And the ARMY has run with it, organizing within their ranks to identify ways they can help those in need. It's typical to see ARMYs rally toward a particular charitable cause to commemorate a BTS milestone, such as the band's

BTS and the Korean Committee for UNICEF announced the launch of the Love Myself initiative, a two-year fund-raising effort to support UNICEF's #ENDviolence program.

anniversary or a member's birthday. In December 2018 they donated $10,000 to the Korean Council for Justice and Remembrance for the Issues of Military Sexual Slavery to aid surviving South Korean "comfort women," those forced to serve in Japanese brothels during World War II. And to celebrate Jin's 26th birthday, fans donated $5,000 worth of sanitary products to low-income females in his hometown of Gwacheon. Fans raised a similar amount for the charity MindLeaps—specifically their efforts in Rwanda—for Jimin's birthday. For J-Hope, fans contributed to a charity that helps repair facial deformities for children in Peru and donated sacks of rice to a food bank in his

A revolving door of hair colors is just one way in which the band members express their individual styles.

hometown of Gwangju. And for the band's fourth anniversary, ARMYs raised $15,000 to aid children with life-threatening diseases. These efforts characterize the ARMY and its willingness to think about the global unity and peace espoused by their idols.

In 2017 BTS made a huge push by partnering with UNICEF to launch the Love Myself campaign against violence toward children around the world. They encouraged people to share their stories of self-love and to share love with others. As of this writing, the hashtag #BTSLoveMyself has been used more than 10 million times, and the effort has raised more than $2 million worldwide. UNICEF director

Henrietta Fore wrote, "The LOVE MYSELF campaign is proof that young people around the world can come together and make a difference. From your music to your messages to your donations, you've shown the power of kindness."

Efforts like this make BTS stand apart from the rest of their peers.

When they speak, people listen. "The first rule is to love ourselves," RM told *Time* in 2018. "Life has many unpredictable issues, problems, dilemmas. But if you admit it…I think the most important thing to live well [is to] be yourself." ♦

A fan in Los Angeles shows off her BTS-inspired tattoo.

RM speaks HIMSELF

RM's speech to the United Nations in 2018 was impactful, empowering, and emotional. It was also a historic moment for the band, which became the first K-pop group ever to stand before the UN. "I was holding the paper…and my hands were shaking," RM recalled to *Good Morning America*. "It was…the best moment in my life."

So what did he say? Read on for the full transcript of his address to the UN's General Assembly.

My name is Kim Nam-joon, also known as RM, the leader of the group BTS. It's an incredible honor to be invited to an occasion with such significance for today's young generation.

Last November, BTS launched the Love Myself campaign with UNICEF, building on our belief that "true love first begins with loving myself." We have been partnering with UNICEF's #ENDviolence program to protect children and young people all over the world from violence. Our fans have become a major part of this campaign with their action and enthusiasm. We truly have the best fans in the world.

I would like to begin by talking about myself. I was born in Ilsan, a city near Seoul, South Korea. It's a beautiful place, with a lake, hills, and even an annual flower festival. I spent a happy childhood there, and I was just an ordinary boy. I

would look up at the night sky in wonder and dream the dreams of a boy. I used to imagine that I was a superhero, saving the world.

In an intro to one of our early albums, there is a line that says, "My heart stopped…I was maybe nine or ten." Looking back, that's when I began to worry about what other people thought of me and started seeing myself through their eyes. I stopped looking up at the stars at night. I stopped daydreaming. I tried to jam myself into molds that other people made. Soon, I began to shut out my own voice and started to listen to the voices of others. No one called out my name, and neither did I. My heart stopped and my eyes closed shut. So, like this, I, we, all lost our names. We became like ghosts.

I had one sanctuary, and that was music. There was a small voice in me that said, "Wake up, man, and listen to yourself!" But it took me a long time to hear music calling my name.

Even after making the decision to join BTS, there were hurdles. Most people thought we were hopeless. Sometimes, I just wanted to quit. I think I was very lucky that I didn't give it all up.

I'm sure that I, and we, will keep stumbling and falling. We have become artists performing in huge stadiums and selling millions of albums. But I am still an ordinary twenty-four-year-old guy. If there's anything that I've achieved, it was only possible because I had my other BTS members by my side, and because of the love and support of our ARMY fans.

Maybe I made a mistake yesterday, but yesterday's me is still me. I am who I am today, with all my faults. Tomorrow I might be a tiny bit wiser, and that's me, too. These faults and mistakes are what I am, making up the brightest stars in the constellation of my life. I have come to love myself for who I was, who I am, and who I hope to become.

I would like to say one last thing. After releasing the Love Yourself albums and launching the Love Myself campaign, we started to hear remarkable stories from our fans all over the world, how our message helped them overcome their hardships in life and start loving themselves. These stories constantly remind us of our responsibility.

So let's all take one more step. We have learned to love ourselves, so now I urge you to speak yourself. I would like to ask all of you. What is your name? What excites you and makes your heart beat? Tell me your story. I want to hear your voice, and I want to hear your conviction. No matter who you are, where you're from, your skin color, gender identity: speak yourself. Find your name, find your voice by speaking yourself.

I'm Kim Nam-joon, RM of BTS. I'm a hip-hop idol and an artist from a small town in Korea. Like most people, I made many mistakes in my life. I have many faults and I have many fears, but I am going to embrace myself as hard as I can, and I'm starting to love myself, little by little.

What is your name? Speak yourself!

K-POP:
A GLOSSARY
OF TERMS

Fans take selcas with cutouts of BTS wearing traditional Korean garb—hanbok—at an exhibit of the 2018 Gangnam Festival.

By now you've had an introduction to the wonderful world of BTS, but so many pleasures still await you. Have you checked out their YouTube channel, BangtanTV? And what about all their music videos? You gotta go way back to their very first song, "No More Dream," to see 'em all. And of course there's Twitter, Facebook, Instagram…the message boards and fan forums…the reality series…their Bangtan Bombs and all that old footage from their musical competitions…their mixtapes and collaborations with other artists…the concert films and livestreams…. Yes, being a fan of BTS is the gift that keeps on giving, and the sensational seven are only one mouse click away.

But first, why don't we brush up on our Korean, shall we? Here are a few essential Korean words and phrases every K-pop fan should know, whether you're planning on visiting Seoul or just communicating with your idol via social media.

Can You Talk the Talk?

aegyo: Acting flirtatious or cutesy, it's especially associated with the flirtatious onstage behavior of idol groups. Jimin's got it in spades with his eye smile.

aigoo: It's an interjection used in surprise, frustration, or chastisement meaning, basically, "Oops."

andwae: No way! As in, "Did BTS just debut another album at No. 1? *Andwae!*"

an moo: Choreography. It's universally considered an essential element of any idol group.

assa: Woo-hoo!

be peu: Like "BFF," it's an abbreviation meaning "best friend."

bi dam: The most attractive member in a group.

chingu: Friend.

choom: Dance.

daebak: Awesome.

dongsaeng: Meaning younger brother or sister, it can be used to refer to anyone younger than oneself.

ganji: Stylish, trendy, fashionable— your everyday, ordinary swag.

gayo: Another name for K-pop.

geumsabba: If you've fallen in love at first sight, this word describes you!

gomawo: Thank you.

gwiyomi: Slang term for someone adorable or cute, often a child.

Fans shop for products in the BT21 collection. BTS launched the effort with Line Friends in 2017, creating avatars for each of the band's seven members.

haeng syo: An informal way to say good-bye, roughly translating to "Peace out."

hoobae: Meaning "junior," it's a respectful term of address for someone younger/more inexperienced than you.

hul: Next time you want to type "I can't even…" try this instead, roughly meaning "whoa."

hyung: Older brother, but can be used to refer to a close friend as well.

hyung line: The senior members in the group. RM, Suga, Jin, and J-Hope comprise BTS's *hyung line*.

jebal: Please.

jjang: Alternately, awesome or the very best.

jon jal: Incredibly good-looking, when referring to a male—as in, "My, is V *jon jal*!"

king wang jjang: If you love BTS infinity squared, try this phrase on for size. It doesn't get any more superlative than this, meaning the absolute best.

maknae: Youngest member of a group; in BTS's case, Jungkook.

maknae line: The younger members in the group—in BTS, V, Jimin, and Jungkook.

manleb: Next level. This is the word you use to describe someone whose skills are way beyond their peers'. (Any ideas, ARMY?)

maum: Emotions, or heart. Warning: a *maum* can be stolen!

mi nam: A handsome guy.

mwongi: The Korean version of "WTF?!"

nam chin: Boyfriend.

omo: Short for *omona*, it means "Oh, my!"

oppa: Older brother, or any male older than oneself.

ottoke: An expression of confusion or exasperation that means "What to do?" As in, "OMG, BTS is playing the same day as my graduation. *Ottoke?*"

saesang: An overly obsessive fan… but not in a good way.

sangnamja: A manly man. As in, "Look at Jungkook's abs—what a *sangnamja*!"

sa rang hae: I love you.

selca: Selfie.

shim koong: Like the feeling you might get seeing your first BTS concert, it means your heart is beating a mile a minute.

K-Pop: A Glossary of Terms

simkung: Translating roughly to "heartthrob," this is how you can refer to your bias.

sunbae: Meaning "senior," it's an honorific that members of BTS would use to address, say, Rain.

ulzzang: A combination of "face" and "best," it is a superlative used to describe a particularly handsome guy.

yeo chin: Girlfriend.

The Modern Language Association reported that there has been a 45 percent increase in Korean language students among American universities in recent years. Could K-pop be the reason?

Great! You've added some Korean to your lexicon. Here are a few more English-language terms to help you talk the talk when it comes to K-pop.

age line: Everyone born in the same year belongs to the same age line. In BTS, Jimin and V are part of the same age line, as are J-Hope and RM.

Bonus: Essential English-language K-pop Terms

all-kill: When a group's song hits No. 1 on all of South Korea's top music charts simultaneously, they've achieved an all-kill.

anti: A hater. Recently, some die-hard EXO fans have shown themselves to be BTS antis.

bias: Your favorite member within a group.

chocolate abs: Picture this—abs so defined they look like a chocolate bar.

comeback: Think of it more like "follow-up." It's a term used to describe a group's latest album. Whenever a new release is issued, it's the group's comeback.

debut: It's what you're thinking. A band makes its official debut when it drops its first album and does the promotional rounds.

eye smile: Fans of *America's Next Top Model* know the "smize." It's pretty self-explanatory.

fighting: Used to cheer on your idols, it's like saying "Go get 'em!"

idol: It's a term used to describe a K-pop group. See BTS's "Idol" for further elaboration.

Koreaboo: A person who has a strong affinity for all things Korean.

leader: Every K-pop act has an official leader. RM exemplifies this role in myriad ways.

Performing on Jimmy Kimmel Live! *in 2017.*

point dance: This describes a difficult piece of a song's choreography, often performed at the beginning of the chorus. Frequently, a band will teach fans the point dance as a way to promote a new song.

rookie: An artist that has just made its debut; the rookie phase generally lasts for the group's first year.

stan: This originated with Eminem's song of the same name, about a violently obsessive fan, though it's come to mean a fan who is devoted in a good way!

trainee: An artist who has yet to make its debut. In K-pop, members train for years before making their official debut.

visual: This term describes the look of the group, how the performance appears onstage. It can also describe the member designated to be the face of the group, often the most attractive. BTS designated Jin for this position, to the delight of many ARMYs.

"We came together with a common dream to write, dance, and produce music that reflects our musical backgrounds as well as our life values of acceptance, vulnerability, and being successful."

—RM to Time